PREACHING ROMANS

PREACHING ROMANS

Four Perspectives

Edited by

Scot McKnight *and* Joseph B. Modica

WILLIAM B. EERDMANS PUBLISHING COMPANY

GRAND RAPIDS, MICHIGAN

Wm. B. Eerdmans Publishing Co.
4035 Park East Court SE, Grand Rapids, Michigan 49546
www.eerdmans.com

28 27 26 25 24 23 22 21 20 19   1 2 3 4 5 6 7 8 9 10

ISBN 978-0-8028-7545-7

Library of Congress Cataloging-in-Publication Data

Names: McKnight, Scot, editor.
Title: Preaching Romans : four perspectives / edited by Scot McKnight and
    Joseph B. Modica.
Description: Grand Rapids : Eerdmans Publishing Co., 2019. | Includes
    bibliographical references and index.
Identifiers: LCCN 2018039048 | ISBN 9780802875457 (pbk. : alk. paper)
Subjects: LCSH: Bible. Romans—Criticism, interpretation, etc. | Bible.
    Romans—Sermons.
Classification: LCC BS2665.52 .P74 2019 | DDC 227/.106—dc23
    LC record available at https://lccn.loc.gov/2018039048

To Joseph's parents,

Frances (†March 5, 2017) and Benjamin (†March 8, 2017) Modica—

for ironing loose-leaf pages of homework

and for the World Book Encyclopedia.

Requiescant in pace.

CONTENTS

ACKNOWLEDGMENTS

We are grateful to all our contributors, who met deadlines, submitted outstanding essays and sermons, and offered keen insights along the way, and to our terrific editors, Michael Thomson, Jenny Hoffman, and Ryan Davis, who shepherded this project to completion.

I (JBM) am grateful to my longtime friend and coeditor, Scot McKnight, for his generous kindness in allowing me to dedicate our volume to my parents, who died within a few days of each other in 2017. It was a difficult time for my brother Steven, my sister Maria, and me as we handled complicated medical decisions. We cried, prayed, cried some more, and consoled each other. It was, to say the least, a family effort.

Two memorable events in my childhood played a part in launching me into scholarship. First, my mother was the epitome of diligence and perfection. While in grade school, I often rushed through my homework to be able to go outside and play with my friends. That usually meant sloppy and crinkled loose-leaf pages of homework. One day my mother, in a moment of exasperation, took out the ironing board, heated up the iron, and began to iron my pages. I couldn't believe my eyes. "You won't hand in anything sloppy anymore, Joseph." I was in second grade. I still remember that day.

Second, my father worked an extra job to be able to purchase a brand-new set of World Book Encyclopedia, those 1960s green-and-white volumes ranging from A to Z. My father also brought a two-tier bookshelf for the encyclopedias. I thought the Library of Congress had arrived at the Modica home! I was in the third grade, and I began to read every volume from cover to cover. Unbeknownst to me, however, my parents realized that the H volume contained male and female human anatomy transparencies. They knew I wasn't ready for "the conversation," so they hid the volume for a while. They each had wisdom and a great sense of humor.

May they both rest in peace.

INTRODUCTION

The apostle Paul's letters remain enigmatic for New Testament interpreters and for those who preach on them. This book fairly presents major interpretive perspectives on Paul and offers insights into how these perspectives influence the preaching of Paul's letters and therefore how these perspectives might affect listeners in the pews.

The interpretation of the Letter to the Romans in particular is contested to such an extent that many pastors have become afraid to preach through Romans. If they are lectionary pastors, they may wander into a designated text, but they know they are wading quickly into deep waters. Many pastors wish they had more time to become familiar with Pauline scholarship and to patiently work through more texts in Romans.

This book provides an accessible sketch of the four major interpretive schools of thought on Paul today: the Reformational (old) perspective, the new perspective, the apocalyptic Paul, and the participationist perspective. Each approach to Paul is written by a leading proponent of that approach. The book then provides three sermons from well-known preachers that illustrate how a particular approach to interpreting Romans might play out in preaching Paul.

In addition to being for pastors, this book is for laypersons who want to know more the interpretive processes on the apostle Paul and Romans in particular, since Paul enjoys unique status in having many lay readers showing interest in academic work on his epistles.

Like the apostle Paul, we hope that your mind will be renewed (Rom. 12:2) by the scholarship and the pastoral sensibilities of this volume.

SCOT McKNIGHT AND JOSEPH B. MODICA

INTERPRETIVE PERSPECTIVES ON THE APOSTLE PAUL

Romans and the "Lutheran" Paul

Stephen Westerholm

Known today simply as an empiricist philosopher, John Locke (1632–1704) was also seen in the past as a careful student of Paul. His *Paraphrase and Notes on the Epistles of St Paul* was widely read throughout the eighteenth century and well into the nineteenth. In the preface to his *Paraphrase*, Locke noted the dangers faced by readers of Paul who consult commentators on the apostle's writings. On the one hand, some consult only those commentators whom they consider "sound and Orthodox." Naturally, they find in those works only what confirms their own opinions: hardly, Locke insisted, the way to arrive at Paul's "true Meaning." On the other hand, there are those who consult a variety of commentators, excluding none "who offers to enlighten them in any of the dark Passages." The problem for these readers is that they emerge from the exercise "distracted with an hundred [interpretations], suggested by those they advised with; and so instead of that one Sense of the Scripture which they carried with them to their Commentators, return from them with none at all." If readers of the first type find their own rather than Paul's intended sense, the latter "find no settled Sense at all."[1]

The quandary in which, according to Locke, readers of diverse commentators found themselves in his day is, if anything, a still greater dilemma for those today who attempt to keep abreast of Pauline scholarship—as the present volume itself amply demonstrates. And yet, if Scripture is to be the final authority for believers' faith and practice, then what it requires them to believe and do must be accessible to them. Protestant talk of *sola scriptura* has always been accompanied by a conviction about Scripture's *perspicuity*: the belief that, *in all that is essential*, the meaning of Scripture is clear to humble believers who approach God's word with a prayer for the illumination of

---

1. John Locke, *A Paraphrase and Notes on the Epistles of St Paul*, 2 vols., ed. Arthur W. Wainwright (Oxford: Clarendon, 1987), 1:108–9 (italics of the original removed).

God's Spirit and a willingness to obey the message they receive.[2] Consistent with this conviction, the argument of this essay is that, in spite of the diverse views propounded by scholars on any number of points of Pauline interpretation, certain fundamental truths are so clearly taught in Scripture (here our focus will be on the Letter to the Romans) that they may—and *ought*—to be affirmed confidently. More specifically, while recent scholarship has rightly drawn attention to the first-century context in which Paul wrote and to elements of his argument that have at times been overlooked, central features of the traditional or "old" perspective on Paul (now often referred to as the "Lutheran perspective") are indisputably Pauline and remain foundational to any proper understanding of the apostle—and, indeed, of the Christian gospel itself. The "central features" here discussed—while due attention is given to Paul's argument in context—are the following:

1. In God's eyes, all human beings are sinful.
2. No human being is righteous in God's eyes on the basis of the deeds they have done.
3. God has provided atonement for the sin of human beings through the death of his Son, Jesus Christ.
4. By God's grace alone, apart from human works, God finds righteous those who have faith in Jesus Christ.

The Universality of Human Sinfulness

For many believers, Romans 3:23 has served (since childhood!) as the primary proof text for universal human sinfulness: "For all have sinned and fall short of the glory of God."[3] When detached (as memory work!) from its context, much that is important to Paul—and most of his argument in the preceding chapters in Romans—is lost to view. Here I will attempt to fill out that picture while at the same time insisting that the common use to which Romans 3:23 has been put is no distortion of Paul.

In Romans 1:16–17, Paul sets forth in summary form the essence of the gospel, "the power of God for salvation." He returns to the topic and

---

2. See Stephen Westerholm and Martin Westerholm, *Reading Sacred Scripture: Voices from the History of Biblical Interpretation* (Grand Rapids: Eerdmans, 2016), 220–21, 267–69, 273–74.

3. Scripture quotations are from the English Standard Version.

develops it two chapters further on, at 3:21. (See the discussion of points 3 and 4 below.) Before doing so, however, he insists on the universal need for the message he proclaims (1:18–3:20). Romans 3:23 may well serve as a summary of his argument (indeed, it serves that purpose in its original context), but students of Paul will want to know the steps he takes before reaching that conclusion.

Readers of Romans 1:18–3:20 can hardly fail to notice that, though the conclusions Paul reaches are universal, he arrives at them after spending a good deal of time discussing the relative standing before God of Jews, on the one hand, and non-Jews (or gentiles), on the other. Indeed, the bulk of his discussion seems less concerned with demonstrating that all are sinners than it is with showing that, differences between them notwithstanding, Jews and gentiles are on the same footing before God. The fundamental principle of "God's righteous judgment" is that God will judge all human beings according to their deeds (2:5–6). Paul spells out the principle in the simplest of terms: God requires, of all human beings, that they do what is "good" and avoid doing what is "evil." He will grant eternal life to those who do what is good, while those who do evil will face his wrath (2:7–10). But even in stating this fundamental principle, Paul is clearly bent on emphasizing its applicability to Jews and "Greeks" (gentiles) alike:

> [God] will render to each one according to his works: to those who by patience in well-doing seek for glory and honor and immortality, he will give eternal life; but for those who are self-seeking and do not obey the truth, but obey unrighteousness, there will be wrath and fury. There will be tribulation and distress for every human being who does evil, *the Jew first and also the Greek*, but glory and honor and peace for everyone who does good, *the Jew first and also the Greek. For God shows no partiality.* (2:6–11)

"The Jew first," because in important respects the Jews have long been a privileged people. But Paul's point here is that the same basic principle of judgment applies to Jews and non-Jews alike—and necessarily so, since "God shows no partiality." His argument then proceeds by taking into account the very real differences between Jews and gentiles and yet showing that there is *no* essential difference when God judges human beings according to their deeds. The principle stands: both will be judged by whether what they have done is "good" or "evil."

The principle of course assumes that Jews and gentiles both *know* the good they are to do and the evil they are to avoid. Against any such simple assumption, the argument might be raised that Jews, but not gentiles, have been given God's law, which spells out what is to be done and what avoided. Paul has no quibble with the premise of that argument (note 2:12, 14, 18, 20); but he insists that, when God judges the deeds of human beings, mere possession of (the written code of) the law makes no difference. It makes no difference because (a) God's demands as found in the law given to Jews are identical with the good that he requires of all human beings; (b) gentiles, though lacking the law given to Jews, are nonetheless aware of the good they must do; and (c) since what God requires is the *doing* of what is good, Jews who possess the written code, no less than gentiles who lack it, must actually *do* the good if God is to find them righteous.

a. In Romans 2:10, Paul insists that Jews and gentiles alike must do "good" if God is to grant them "glory and honor and peace" (the equivalent of the "eternal life" mentioned in 2:7). In 2:13, however, the language has changed: in *this* verse, what God requires of those he will find righteous is that they be "doers of the law." Yet Paul is still thinking of what God requires of Jews and gentiles alike, for he proceeds to show how gentiles, though not in possession of the written law, can nonetheless be held responsible for doing "what the law requires" (2:14; see [b] below). His argument thus rests on the assumption that what the *law* commands people to do (2:13) is the same as the *good* that, according to 2:10, God requires of all human beings.[4] Two points about this assumption are worth noting.

First, in speaking of what the law requires, Paul is not, for the moment at least, thinking of what are commonly called the "ceremonial" demands of the law; after all, he makes abundantly clear elsewhere that he does *not* think gentiles are required to observe Jewish feasts or food laws, or that gentile males should be circumcised (e.g., Gal. 4:10–11; 5:2–6). Rather, the prohibitions of stealing and adultery, mentioned later in the chapter, represent the kind of commandment he has in mind (Rom. 2:21–22).

---

4. The same understanding is reflected in Rom. 5:13 ("sin indeed was in the world before the law was given") and 4:15 ("where there is no law there is no transgression"). What is right was right, and what is wrong was wrong (it was *sin*), even before the law was given. Cain *sinned* when he murdered Abel; but he did not *transgress* the commandment "You shall not murder" (Exod. 20:13) because that commandment had not yet been given. The giving of the law turned what was already *sin* (e.g., murder) into *transgression*, the breaking of an explicit commandment (in the case of murder, the sixth). That the law spells out what is good is evident as well in Rom. 7:12, 16; 13:8–10.

Second, the notion that the demands of the Mosaic law code spell out the good that God requires of all human beings was widely held by Jews of Paul's day. If Proverbs speaks of "wisdom" as that which human beings (*all* human beings) are to pursue and practice (Prov. 3:13–18; 4:5–9, etc.), later Jewish literature identified this "wisdom" with the law given by God to Moses on Mount Sinai (e.g., Sir. 24:1–27). In Jewish apologetic literature, this conviction took on a particular shape: given that, in the Greco-Roman world, philosophers often stated ethical ideals in terms of conformity with "nature" or "the [unwritten] law of nature," Jewish apologists were wont to speak of the Mosaic law as the perfect embodiment of "the law of nature." After all, they reasoned, the divine Source of the law of nature can be none other than the God who gave Israel his law; inevitably, then, the order of nature is reflected in the prescriptions of the Mosaic law (see 4 Macc. 5:25–26).

In short, Paul need anticipate no disagreement when he identifies the good that God requires of all human beings with the (moral) demands of the Mosaic law.

b. He does, however, anticipate the objection that gentiles can hardly be held responsible for keeping a law they have not been given. Granting that gentiles are those "who do not have the law," he uses the self-evident fact that gentiles at times do what the law requires (e.g., refrain from murder, adultery, and theft) to show that God has given them an inner awareness of the law's basic demands (2:14–15).[5] Coming immediately after the declaration that "the doers of the law" will be "justified" (2:13), this insistence that gentiles are aware of the good required in the law (2:14–15) serves to place gentiles effectively on the same footing as Jews in the face of divine judgment (2:16): both must do the good—and that is what the law requires.

c. The *form* in which Jews encounter God's basic requirements—a written law code—permits no doubt or discussion regarding their content. "Instructed from the law," the very "embodiment of knowledge and truth," Jews "know [God's] will"; indeed, they consider themselves able to instruct gentiles about the good that God requires of them both ("you are sure that you yourself are a guide to the blind, a light to those who are in dark-

---

5. Paul is not here positing the existence of righteous gentiles: so much is clear from the way he goes on to speak of the thoughts of these same gentiles who "do what the law requires" as "accus[ing] or even excus[ing] them" (2:15; his language implies that accusing is more likely than excusing!). His point is simply that whenever gentiles, who have not been given the written code of the law, nonetheless observe particular demands of the law, they prove their awareness of the good God requires of them.

ness, an instructor of the foolish, a teacher of children") (2:17–20). Without denying that Jews, in possession of the law, are a privileged people, Paul proceeds to press *his* point: Jews and gentiles stand on the same footing before God's righteous judgment. He has shown that gentiles cannot be excused from the requirement of doing what is good, since they too have a God-given awareness of what God demands. Starting at 2:21, he emphasizes that possession of (the written code of) the law does not excuse Jews from the requirement (shared with gentiles!) of actually *doing* the good commanded by the law.

Jews and Gentiles Stand on the Same Footing

The apostle begins by rhetorically asking an imaginary Jew whether he in fact keeps the commandments he teaches to others: "You then who teach others, do you not teach yourself? While you preach against stealing, do you steal? You who say that one must not commit adultery, do you commit adultery? You who abhor idols, do you rob temples?" (2:21–22). Note that Paul is not *charging* Jews with stealing, committing adultery, or robbing temples;[6] his question *whether* they do so merely stresses that the crucial issue is not what one knows and can teach others but whether one, in practice, measures up to what one knows and teaches.

That Paul is not here charging Jews with transgressing the law but merely reminding them that obedience, not possession, of the law is what matters is apparent from the words that follow immediately: "Circumcision indeed is of value if you obey the law." The (theoretical) possibility that Jews observe the law is evidently still on the table. So too is the alternative: "but if you break the law, your circumcision becomes uncircumcision" (2:25). Here what distinguishes Jews from gentiles is no longer possession of (the written code of) the law but circumcision, the external mark of the people of God. But Paul's point remains the same: before God's judgment, what matters—for Jews and non-Jews alike—is the actual *doing* of what the law requires: "So, if a man who is uncircumcised keeps the precepts of the law,

---

6. Those who think he is doing so then wonder how fair Paul's charge can be: did Jews typically rob temples? (Even if the odd Jew did so, surely such occurrences were so rare as to make Paul's words, understood as a *general* charge against Jews, unjustified.) In fact, this extreme example Paul chooses serves most effectively to make his point: surely no one thinks robbing temples can be excused because thieves know that the law forbids their doing so! It follows, then, that knowledge of the law apart from its observance is worthless.

will not his uncircumcision be regarded as circumcision? Then he who is physically uncircumcised but keeps the law will condemn you who have the written code and circumcision but break the law" (2:26–27).

Again, Paul is not saying that there *are* circumcised Jews "who obey the law," on the one hand (2:25a), or Jews who "break the law," on the other (2:25b); nor is he saying that there *are* uncircumcised gentiles who "keep the precepts of the law" (2:26). Whether or not such people exist is of no relevance to his argument, the thrust of which—as throughout chapter 2—is to establish the *principle* that the actual *doing* of what God requires is what matters for Jews and gentiles alike. That gentiles lack the written code of the law and circumcision does not excuse them from their responsibility to *do* what is good. Jews, who possess the written code of the law and circumcision, share the same responsibility. At the divine judgment, the same standard—the requirement of righteous *deeds*—is demanded of both. *That* is the point of Romans 2.

Still, the universal sinfulness of humankind—and hence the universal need for the gospel of Jesus Christ—is the ultimate conclusion Paul reaches based on the argument of 1:18–3:20. *That* point was made already in 1:18–32, which denounced "all ungodliness and unrighteousness" of human beings; it is confirmed by the quotations from Scripture in 3:10–18. "All have sinned," and all need "the righteousness of God" revealed in Jesus Christ: that, in the end, *is* Paul's point in 1:18–3:20. But our understanding of Romans is enhanced when his whole argument is taken into account: "For there is no distinction [between Jews and gentiles, in this respect]: for all have sinned" (3:22–23). This context, stressed in modern scholarship, is important for Paul. But Paul's insistence on the universal sinfulness of humankind is clear, as it has always been clear, to every reader of Romans.

One other, related emphasis of modern scholarship should here be noted. Scholars today frequently stress that, whereas Romans 1–3 portrays the human dilemma in terms of the *sins* (plural) that people commit, Romans 5–7 depicts the dilemma in terms of slavery to *sin* (singular). Whereas students of Paul of an earlier day may have focused on *sins* and the need for justification (treating the "doctrine of justification" as the center of Paul's thought), the tendency of many scholars today is to see the "true Paul" as more (if not exclusively) concerned with humanity's enslavement to the power of *sin* and need for liberation. Such distinctions between Romans 1–3 and 5–7 are, I believe, too sharply drawn in any case. On the one hand, Paul speaks already in Romans 3:9 of Jews and gentiles alike as being "under [the power of] sin [singular]." In Romans 1, he clearly sees the individual *sins* (plural; examples are listed later in the chapter) that people commit as further expressions of the fundamental *sin* of refusing to give God due honor and thanks (1:21). And that fundamental sin has so rendered their thinking vain and their hearts darkened (1:21–22) that we can, in effect, speak of a slavery to sin already in chapter 1. On the other hand, it is clear in Romans 6 that slavery to sin and the giving of oneself to practice particular sins follow from each other (see 6:12–19). We may allow the Johannine Jesus to make Paul's point: "Everyone who practices sin is a slave to sin" (John 8:34). Universal sinfulness, reflecting a slavery to sin and expressed in the committing of particular sins, remains a fundamental Pauline conviction.

But to return to our point: in Paul's first-century context, the claim that all human beings are sinners (indeed, slaves of sin) in need of the gospel had to be accompanied by an insistence that the divine requirement to *do* what is good applies to Jews and non-Jews alike. That context, important to Paul and to the argument of the opening chapters of Romans, is lost to view when Romans 3:23 is detached from its context. Still, it is no distortion of Paul to point to the universal sinfulness of humankind as the dilemma to which the gospel brings the divine solution.

The Inadequacy of "Good Works"

We naturally associate negative talk about "good works" with Martin Luther—not entirely fairly, since Luther wrote a fine "Treatise on Good Works" and always insisted on their importance in the life of a believer: where true faith is present, good works cannot fail to be found; where good works are lacking, true faith is not to be found.[7] But Luther also insisted that where true faith is not found, neither can there be any (truly) good works. Just as we must have apple trees before we can have apples, so people (sinners that they are) must be made good before they can produce good works.[8] "Flesh" (untransformed human nature) can only produce the works of the flesh (John 3:6), and these (even if we are speaking of the highest morality of which the world is capable), in the absence of faith, are unacceptable to God.[9] And yet, Luther believes, the notion that God's favor can be gained

7. See Martin Luther, *Lectures on Galatians: 1535*, in *Luther's Works*, vol. 27, ed. Jaroslav Pelikan (Saint Louis: Concordia, 1964), 30.

8. See Martin Luther, *Lectures on Galatians: 1535*, in *Luther's Works*, vol. 26, ed. Jaroslav Pelikan (Saint Louis: Concordia, 1963), 169, 255.

9. See Luther, *Lectures on Galatians*, 26:139–40, 216.

by the good works we do is "the fundamental principle of the devil and of the world."[10] "There is no difference at all between a papist, a Jew, a Turk, or a sectarian. Their persons, locations, rituals, religions, works, and forms of worship are, of course, diverse; but they all have the same reason, the same heart, the same opinion and idea. . . . 'If I do this or that, I have a God who is favorably disposed toward me; if I do not, I have a God who is wrathful.'"[11]

At this point, many modern scholars think Luther and his followers are guilty of misreading Paul on two counts. First, the Jews of Paul's day were not *legalists* who imagined that they were earning, or could earn, salvation by their own deeds; they relied on God's grace no less than Paul did. The second point follows from the first: when Paul says that no one can be justified by "works of the law" (Rom. 3:20; Gal. 2:16), he is not attacking the notion that people could earn their salvation by good deeds—an issue he never confronted. He *was* confronted by the question of whether gentile believers needed to be circumcised and keep Jewish food and festival laws. The point, then, of Romans 3:20 and Galatians 2:16 is that *such* "works of the law" are not the basis for justification. Paul's target was Jewish *ethnocentrism*, the notion that gentiles had to become Jews to be saved.

Again, it must be said that modern scholars have rightly reminded us of the context within which Paul was writing and the issue he faced. And yet again, it should be perfectly clear that Luther's insistence that no one can be righteous in God's sight by the good deeds they do is no distortion of Paul. This is not the place to address the issue of Jewish reliance on grace.[12] To my mind, the debate between traditional scholars who claim that Paul is attacking Jewish legalism and those today who claim his target is rather Jewish ethnocentrism has itself distorted Paul's argument. When Paul denies that people can be righteous by the law and its "works," his point is not that Jews have distorted the law in a legalistic way, thinking (self-righteously) that their obedience to the law gives them a claim on God, who must recognize them as righteous; nor is his point that Jews, thinking ethnocentrically, have distorted the law by claiming that non-Jews must become Jews and keep the distinctively Jewish parts of the law if they are to be justified. He is not in fact attacking Jewish distortions of the law at all. He is insisting that

---

10. Luther, *Lectures on Galatians*, 27:146.

11. Luther, *Lectures on Galatians*, 26:396.

12. For such discussion, see my *Perspectives Old and New on Paul: The "Lutheran" Paul and His Critics* (Grand Rapids: Eerdmans, 2004), 341–51; *Justification Reconsidered: Rethinking a Pauline Theme* (Grand Rapids: Eerdmans, 2013), 23–34; and especially John M. G. Barclay, *Paul and the Gift* (Grand Rapids: Eerdmans, 2015).

the law itself—as given, and rightly understood—spells out what people ought to do; accordingly, by the standards of the law, those who do what the law commands are righteous. Conversely, for those who have *not* kept its commands, the law cannot serve as the path to righteousness.

Paul finds the basic principle of the law in Leviticus 18:5, which he quotes in Romans 10:5: "For Moses writes about the righteousness that is based on the law, that the person who does the commandments shall live by them" (so also Gal. 3:12). (This, be it noted, is *Moses* speaking, and in sacred Scripture; it *cannot* be, for Paul, a "legalistic" distortion of what the law is all about.) The law indeed "promised life"—to those who obey its demands (Rom. 7:10). In these verses, those who "live" (or have "life") are surely those who enjoy God's favor in this life and the next; the same point, then, is being made in Paul's own words when he writes that it is "the doers of the law who will be justified" (Rom. 2:13). By its very nature, the law, made up of commandments, tells people what they ought to do: as Paul notes, it calls for "doers." And those who do the deeds (we may say, the "works") it requires will be found righteous and live: that is the principle by which the law operates. It is "the righteousness that is based on the law" (Rom. 10:5; cf. Phil. 3:9).[13]

Crucially, however, the same law that promises blessing and life for those who meet its demands also warns that a curse and death follow disobedience.

> See, I have set before you today life and good, death and evil. If you obey the commandments of the LORD your God that I command you today, . . . then you shall live and multiply, and the LORD your God will bless you in the land that you are entering to take possession of it. But if your heart turns away, and you will not hear, . . . I declare to you today, that you shall surely perish. . . . I call heaven and earth to witness against you today that I have set before you life and death, blessing and curse. (Deut. 30:15–19)

When Paul, then, speaks of the covenant under which the law was given as one of "death" and "condemnation" without even mentioning its promise of life for those who meet its demands (2 Cor. 3:7, 9), the point must be that the law's demands have not been met. That *is* the point of Galatians 3:10:

---

13. Cf. Deut. 6:25: "It will be righteousness for us, if we are careful to do all this commandment before the LORD our God, as he has commanded us."

those whose claim to righteousness is based on the "works of the law" are "under a curse; for it is written, 'Cursed be everyone who does not abide by all things written in the Book of the Law, and do them.'" To be sure, Paul is countering, in Galatians, the claim that gentile believers ought to be circumcised and keep Jewish food and festival laws; but when he insists that "by works of the law no one will be justified" (Gal. 2:16), his point (as the whole argument of Galatians makes clear) is that, by getting circumcised, gentiles enter a covenant that requires obedience to the whole law (5:3), a covenant that can only bring *sinners* a curse and death—and why would anyone want to do that? The law cannot give life to dead people, or serve the unrighteous as the path to righteousness. "If a law had been given that could give life, then righteousness would indeed be by the law. But the Scripture imprisoned everything under sin, so that the promise by faith in Jesus Christ might be given to those who believe" (Gal. 3:21–22). Indeed, "if righteousness were through the law, then Christ died for no purpose" (Gal. 2:21). But Christ did die, and died for a purpose ("for our sins" [Gal. 1:4]). For sinful human beings, then, "justification" is *not* "through the law."

And that is the point in Romans 3:20 as well, where Paul again insists that "by works of the law no human being will be justified in his sight."[14] In Romans, the dictum follows (curiously, in the eyes of some readers) the statement that it is "the doers of the law who will be justified" (2:13). But there is no contradiction. Of *course* God would find righteous any who kept his law's commands. But those who do not—and Paul has just stated that Jews and gentiles alike are "under sin" and that "none is righteous, no, not one" (3:9–10)—cannot be justified by "works of the law" that they have not done.

If the question is raised why God bothered giving a law as a purported path to righteousness and life when in fact no human being attains righteousness or life by its means, the answer—based on what we have already seen—should be obvious. The law simply "tells it like it is." It did not *make*

---

14. It is worth pointing out that the argument (beginning at Rom. 1:18) that leads to the conclusion of 3:20 nowhere critiques Jewish legalism, or any self-righteous boast on the part of Jews that they have fulfilled the law and that God must acknowledge their righteousness. The problem is simply that Jews and gentiles alike have *not* done what they ought to do. If by Jewish "ethnocentrism" we mean the assumption that being a (circumcised) Jew, in possession of the law, is sufficient to secure God's favor, then the argument of Rom. 2 certainly undermines such ethnocentrism; but, in the end, Paul's argument that Jews no less than gentiles are sinners is based on the claim that Jews have transgressed the law, not ethnocentrically misunderstood it.

murder, or adultery, or theft wrong. With or without the law, murder, adultery, and theft are wrong—and they are wrong whether no human being murders, commits adultery, or steals, or whether everyone does so. The law merely spells out what is inherently right and wrong, good and evil, in the world as created by God's wisdom. Furthermore, any who do what is right will be found righteous in God's sight—obviously! The basic principle of the law is a simple statement of what makes the world go round, morally speaking. It remains true whether in fact every human being keeps the law or no one does so. We must not treat as normal a race in rebellion against its Creator, even if it is the only race we know: it remains a race gone wrong. In spelling out, for such a race, what is good and what is evil and the inevitable consequences of each, God was making unmistakably clear to them what they, through their God-given moral sensibilities, already knew (note Rom. 1:32)—though in *their* case, the law effectively served not to point out the path to life, but to make still more evident the culpability of their sin (3:20; 4:15; 7:13).

It remains to point out that, *since* no human being can be righteous in God's sight by the works of the law, and *since* the works of the law amount to the good that God requires of all human beings, it follows that no human can be righteous in God's sight *by the good deeds they do*. This "Lutheran" insistence is no distortion of Paul (it is, in fact, the explicit point of Eph. 2:8–9; Titus 3:4–7), even though the immediate issue confronting the apostle in Galatia was whether gentiles should submit to Jewish law.

Atonement for Sin

In the extraordinary situation where a race is in a state of rebellion against its Creator, and where not a single member of the race is righteous (in the ordinary sense of the word) by having done what they ought, God has intervened in an extraordinary way. He has provided atonement for human sin through the death of his Son. God has put Christ Jesus "forward as a propitiation by his blood" (Rom. 3:25).

The word translated "propitiation" (*hilastērion*) by the English Standard Version (NIV, NRSV: "sacrifice of atonement") is much debated. Paul *cannot* mean that Christ, by his death, appeased a God otherwise bent on punishing sinners for their sin: after all, he says explicitly that God himself is the one who has provided the *hilastērion*. If the idea of "propitiation" is retained in Paul's usage, the point can only be that a righteous God, who by his very nature is opposed to sin and must condemn it, has—in his love for sinful human beings (cf. Rom. 5:8)—provided atonement for people's sins so that he need not, after all, condemn them. His opposition to sin is both unmistakably expressed and fully satisfied by the death of Christ, bearing the judgment that our sins deserve (cf. 1 John 2:2; 1 Pet. 2:24).

Paul makes clear that God's righteousness would indeed have been compromised had he chosen merely to overlook sin; indeed, his righteousness *appeared* to be compromised by the way he had failed to prosecute sins in the past, before Christ came: to take but one example, Abraham remained a "friend of God" in spite of obvious sins. In fact, however, God was not *overlooking* but temporarily "passing over" sins: he intended all along that Christ would provide for their atonement. Christ's death thus served the further purpose of demonstrating God's righteousness. "God put forward [Christ Jesus] as a propitiation by his blood, to be received by faith. This was to show God's righteousness, because in his divine forbearance he had passed over former sins. It was to show his righteousness at the present time, so that he might be just and the justifier of the one who has faith in Jesus" (Rom. 3:25–26).

An alternative rendering of the word *hilastērion* is "mercy seat," since the same word is used in the Greek translation of the Old Testament at Leviticus 16:14 (and elsewhere) for the cover of the ark of the covenant on which, on the Day of Atonement, blood was sprinkled as a rite of atonement. Whether or not we should translate *hilastērion* as "mercy seat" in Romans 3:25, that usage of the term suggests the answer to a question sometimes posed as a problem for Paul's understanding of the law: How can Paul claim that sin prevents the law from serving as a path to righteousness when the law itself provides means (such as the Day of Atonement) for atonement? In the light of Romans 3:25, Paul's answer would appear to be the same as that of the Letter to the Hebrews: Old Testament rites of atonement could not, by their very nature, really atone for sins ("For it is impossible for the blood of bulls and goats to take away sins" [Heb. 10:4]); they merely foreshadowed the effective work of Christ, the true "mercy seat," or place of atonement (see Heb. 10:1, 11–12; that Paul thinks along these lines is suggested as well by 1 Cor. 5:7 and Col. 2:16–17).

Paul has traditionally been interpreted as claiming that Christ provided atonement for human sins. He has, in short, been read as saying what he actually says.

By Grace, through Faith

Salvation is "by grace" and "through faith": this assertion of Ephesians 2:8 is amply supported by Paul's argument in his Letter to the Romans.

After Paul has shown, in Romans 1:18–3:20, that no human being is righteous in God's eyes by having met the law's requirements (or done what is "good"), it follows that, if any *are* to be found righteous ("justified"), it will only be "by [God's] grace as a gift" (3:24). Paul immediately proceeds to show how God can righteously declare *sinners* righteous by speaking of how God has provided, in Christ, atonement for their sins (3:25–26). Naturally, those found righteous only because they have received righteousness as a gift of grace, made possible by what Christ has done, have themselves no grounds for boasting (3:27–28).

The "free gift of righteousness" is explicitly mentioned in 5:17 as well, in a context that has already spoken of "the grace of God and the free gift by the grace of that one man Jesus Christ" as bringing "justification" (5:15–16). Those thus found righteous by grace now live where grace is said to "reign" (replacing the "reign" of sin [5:21]; cf. the "grace in which we stand" [5:2]).[15] That a standing before God based on divine grace excludes human "works" as a factor is clear in 11:5–6: "There is a remnant, chosen by grace. But if it is by grace, it is no longer on the basis of works; otherwise grace would no longer be grace."[16]

But a gift must be received: Paul speaks of "those who receive the abundance of grace and the free gift of righteousness" (5:17). Elsewhere in Romans openness to receiving God's gift of righteousness is spoken of as *faith*, which is everywhere regarded as the only viable path to justification.

15. In Rom. 6, Paul explains the disastrous consequences that follow for those who imagine that living "under grace" allows them to continue in sin; so also Rom. 8:13; Gal. 5:13–21.

16. The principle that God constitutes his people without regard to their works is explicit at 9:10–11 and underlies the argument of 9:30–32; 10:6–9; 11:7, 22. Paul's understanding of divine grace as excluding human "works" was not the standard view in Judaism; cf. E. P. Sanders, *Paul and Palestinian Judaism* (Philadelphia: Fortress, 1977), 297: "Grace and works were not considered as opposed to each other in any way. I believe it is safe to say that the notion that God's grace is in any way contradictory to human endeavour is totally foreign to Palestinian Judaism. The reason for this is that grace and works were not considered alternative roads to salvation." Paul's more radical view of human sinfulness was no doubt a factor in his belief that human beings can contribute nothing to their salvation; but Rom. 9 makes clear that it belongs to the very *modus operandi* of God's call and grace to exclude human works (see esp. 9:11, 16; also the literature cited in note 12 above).

For in [the gospel] the righteousness of God is revealed from faith for faith, as it is written, "The righteous shall life by faith." (1:17)

But now the righteousness of God has been manifested apart from the law, although the Law and the Prophets bear witness to it—the righteousness of God through faith in Jesus Christ for all who believe. (3:21–22)[17]

God put forward [Christ Jesus] as a propitiation by his blood, to be received by faith . . . so that he might be just and the justifier of the one who has faith in Jesus. (3:25–26)

We hold that one is justified by faith apart from works of the law. . . . [God] will justify the circumcised by faith and the uncircumcised through faith. (3:28, 30)

To the one who does not work but believes in him who justifies the ungodly, his faith is counted as righteousness. (4:5)

[Abraham] received the sign of circumcision as a seal of the righteousness that he had by faith while he was still uncircumcised. The purpose was to make him the father of all who believe without being circumcised, so that righteousness would be counted to them as well, and to make him the father of the circumcised who are not merely

---

17. The view has become popular of late (due in significant measure to its adoption in Karl Barth's commentary) that Paul speaks of "the faithfulness of Jesus Christ" rather than of "faith in Jesus Christ" in 3:22, and of "the faithfulness of Jesus" rather than of "faith in Jesus" in 3:26. Taken by themselves, the words permit either translation. To my mind, the lively debate on this topic is of little if any significance for our understanding of Paul. Those who insist on the translation "the faithfulness of Jesus (Christ)" must allow that there are other texts where the need for human faith is unmistakable. Those who see Paul as speaking of "faith in Jesus (Christ)" agree wholeheartedly that apart from the (faithful) obedience of Christ, justification would not be possible (cf. Rom. 5:19; Phil. 2:8). The question is simply whether, in ambiguous texts, Paul is in fact speaking of Christ's faithfulness or human faith. Since, in the unambiguous texts related to justification, Paul refers consistently to the faith of the person justified and never to Christ's "faithfulness"—indeed, that "Abraham believed God, and it was counted to him as righteousness" is seen by Paul, throughout Rom. 4 and Gal. 3, as the prototype of the justification of believers in Christ (but see also Rom. 5:1 following 4:24; 10:10)—it seems best, to my mind, to interpret the ambiguous texts accordingly.

circumcised but who also walk in the footsteps of the faith that our father Abraham had before he was circumcised. (4:11–12)

[Abraham's] faith was "counted to him as righteousness." But the words "it was counted to him" were not written for his sake alone, but for ours also. It will be counted to us who believe in him who raised from the dead Jesus our Lord. . . . Therefore, since we have been justified by faith . . . (4:22–5:1)

With the heart one believes and is justified. (10:10)

Indeed, Paul calls the righteousness he speaks of the "righteousness of faith" (4:13), "a righteousness that is by faith" (9:30), "the righteousness based on faith" (10:6); he contrasts it with the (nonviable path to) "righteousness that is based on the law" (10:5; see also Gal. 3:11–12; Phil. 3:9).

Given that Paul sees faith as essential, many have wondered whether faith is not, after all, a human "work" that God requires of those he will justify. Clearly, Paul does not see it so: "Now to the one who works, his wages are not counted as a gift but as his due. And to the one who *does not work but believes in* him who justifies the ungodly, his faith is counted as righteousness" (4:4–5).[18] Later in the same chapter Paul notes that the reception of God's promise "depends on faith" precisely in order that it may "rest on grace" (4:16): like soup and sandwich, faith and grace go together; "works" and grace do not (11:6). Faith is the appropriate response to divine grace; but it is *only* a response. Faith is not, for Paul, a quality inherent in the individual who believes, but a trust in God evoked by hearing God's promise (4:18–21) or the call of Christ in the gospel: "So faith comes from hearing, and hearing through the word of Christ" (10:17). It represents a clinging to God's word by those helpless without it: an aged, childless husband of an aged, barren wife—who had been promised a child (4:18–21); the "weak" and "ungodly," "sinners" at enmity with God (5:6–10)—who will escape God's condemnation only if God, for Christ's sake, declares them righteous. Only God can remedy these situations beyond all human hope (4:18): faith trusts that God will.

It is, then, entirely consistent with the message of Romans to say that, in God's sight, all human beings are sinful; that God requires that we do

---

18. Note too that although Eph. 2:8–9 sees salvation as "through faith," it still claims that it is "not your own doing" and not "of works."

what is good but finds no one good by that criterion; that God has provided, through the atoning death of his Son, atonement for sin; and that God, by his grace, declares sinners righteous who respond with faith to the gospel. Today there is not a trace of novelty in any of these claims. But those who would remain true to the message of the apostles may proclaim them still.

2

Romans and the New Perspective

Scot McKnight

When I watch white nationalists trumpeting their hatred, when I read of racial violence against black men in Chicago by law enforcement, when I observe low-paying, hard-working jobs performed by Latin Americans, when I hear stories about Northern Ireland and the Republic of Ireland, when I study the genocide of Rwanda, and you can add your own systemic injustices against groups of people, I am grateful for what the new perspective on Paul brings to the preacher of Romans. The new perspective's reorientation of all things Pauline through the lens of Galatians 3:28 fires my desire for reconciliation in our world today. Reconciliation needs to begin in the church, and preaching Romans is the place to start.

There are some basic commonalities in every reading of Paul's magnificent Letter to the Romans.[1] The God of Romans is the God of Israel made manifest in the incarnation of Jesus Christ; the God of Israel is the Creator; the covenant God made with Abraham and renewed with Moses and David comes to fulfillment in the new covenant; Jesus is the Messiah, the one promised in Israel's story; the story of Jesus is the center of Israel's, and therefore all creation's, story; the story of Jesus reworks the whole story; the redemption that comes to believers in the Jesus-as-Messiah story is an act of God's grace; we participate in that redemption in faith, love, and obedience; this participation is transformational because the Spirit that makes that redemption actual has been unleashed in the church, the people of God that expands Israel into a worldwide community of Jews and gentiles; the locus of that participation is the church, the *ekklesia*, of Jesus that gathers to worship God in Christ and to indwell one another in

---

1. Cf. Michael J. Gorman, *Apostle of the Crucified Lord: A Theological Introduction to Paul and His Letters*, 2nd ed. (Grand Rapids: Eerdmans, 2016), 183.

I am grateful to Mike Bird for his reading of this chapter.

fellowship through the Spirit, and that engages in mission in this world in a Christoform (or cruciform) life for both individuals and the *ekklesia*. Each believer, then, is summoned by the gospel about Jesus as Messiah to live a life marked by love, grace, forgiveness, justice, peace, and reconciliation. These separable elements, each of which rises to the surface in Romans, are common elements to all perspectives on Paul.

Where to Begin?

Surely E. P. Sanders's *Paul and Palestinian Judaism* created the new perspective, but he had predecessors, beginning with scholars with appreciation for Judaism and sensitivity to articulating Judaism in ways organic to Judaism itself.[2] In other words, with scholars who did not let the categories of Christian theology reshape Judaism, like George Foot Moore and Krister Stendahl.[3] Decisive in this return to Jewish sources were the Holocaust, the discovery of the Dead Sea Scrolls, and the publication of other Jewish texts. Alongside this was the opening of departments of religion in universities and the subsequent development of serious scholarship on religion (which is the door that opened for Sanders). If these elements prepared the way for Sanders, others followed in his steps, in some ways completing his program but in other ways diverging from his approach. Building on Sanders was James D. G. Dunn, who followed up Sanders's "participationist eschatology" with his own approach to Paul.[4] Alongside Dunn was the mushrooming of

2. E. P. Sanders, *Paul and Palestinian Judaism: A Comparison of Patterns of Religion* (Philadelphia: Fortress, 1977). For Sanders's own perspective on his work, see E. P. Sanders, *Comparing Judaism and Christianity: Common Judaism, Paul, and the Inner and the Outer in Ancient Religion* (Minneapolis: Fortress, 2016), 1–27. For his fuller effort on Judaism, see E. P. Sanders, *Judaism: Practice and Belief, 63 BCE–66 CE* (Minneapolis: Fortress, 2016).

3. George Foot Moore, "Christian Writers on Judaism," *Havard Theological Review* 14 (1921): 197–254; George Foot Moore, *Judaism in the First Centuries of the Christian Era: The Age of the Tannaim*, 3 vols. (New York: Schocken Books, 1971); Krister Stendahl, *Paul among Jews and Gentiles and Other Essays* (Philadelphia: Fortress, 1976).

4. James D. G. Dunn, "The New Perspective on Paul," in *The New Perspective on Paul*, rev. ed. (Grand Rapids: Eerdmans, 2008), 99–120. Dunn's works are numerous: *Jesus, Paul and the Law: Studies in Mark and Galatians* (Louisville: Westminster John Knox, 1990); *The Epistle to the Galatians*, Black's New Testament Commentary (Peabody, MA: Hendrickson, 1993); *The Theology of Paul the Apostle* (Grand Rapids: Eerdmans, 1998); *The New Perspective on Paul*; *Romans*, Word Biblical Commentary 38 (Grand Rapids: Zondervan, 2015). Dunn has a short "commentary" on Romans: "Letter to the Romans," in *Dictionary*

new perspective theories on Paul by N. T. Wright.[5] Many scholars have embraced Sanders's covenantal nomism (see below) and taken his insights in other directions for comprehending the apostle Paul. Diversity aside, there are three *R*s in the new perspective: reaction, renewal, and reformulation.

Reaction

The potency of Sanders's *Paul and Palestinian Judaism* came from its polemical edge. Sanders contended that far too many Christian scholars badly misunderstood Judaism and as a result badly misunderstood the apostle Paul: Judaism was redefined not as a works-righteousness religion but as a grace-based religion, which he named "covenantal nomism." Which is to say, one did not obey the law (nomism) to *enter* the covenant (obedience earning salvation) but instead, on the basis of grace and God's covenantal favor (Gen. 12; 15), to *maintain* one's covenant standing.[6]

If Judaism's pattern of religion was covenantal nomism, then many had badly misconstrued Judaism as a works-based religion. One still encounters this pre-Sanders theory of Judaism in sermons in which we hear that humans are by nature works-shaped or seeking to earn favor with God, or which pose religion (read: Judaism) against grace. My point is not that humans aren't egocentric but that such a view is often unconsciously (or at times even consciously) rooted in a way of framing Judaism itself, the foil of the gospel of grace in Paul. Sanders attacked this view of Judaism by examining the evidence with skill. He argued that Christian scholars, theologians, pastors, and laypeople described Christianity as fundamen-

---

of Paul and His Letters, ed. Gerald F. Hawthorne, Ralph P. Martin, and Daniel G. Reid (Downers Grove, IL: InterVarsity Press, 1993), 838–50, esp. 844–50.

5. Wright, too, has numerous works of importance in this discussion: *The Climax of the Covenant: Christ and the Law in Pauline Theology* (Minneapolis: Fortress, 1993); *The New Testament and the People of God*, Christian Origins and the Question of God 1 (Minneapolis: Fortress, 1992); "The Letter to the Romans," in *The New Interpreter's Bible*, vol. 12 (Nashville: Abingdon, 2002), 393–770; *Paul: In Fresh Perspective* (Minneapolis: Fortress, 2009); *Justification: God's Plan and Paul's Vision* (Downers Grove, IL: IVP Academic, 2009); *Pauline Perspectives: Essays on Paul, 1978–2013* (Minneapolis: Fortress, 2013); *Paul and the Faithfulness of God*, 2 vols., Christian Origins and the Question of God 4 (Minneapolis: Fortress, 2013); *Paul and His Recent Interpreters* (Minneapolis: Fortress, 2015).

6. Sanders has responded to his critics: see Sanders, *Comparing Judaism and Christianity*, 51–83; also *Judaism*, 430–51. John Barclay presses Sanders's view of grace beyond its priority: see John M. G. Barclay, *Paul and the Gift* (Grand Rapids: Eerdmans, 2015), 151–58.

tally *antithetical* to Judaism. In essence, Sanders evaluated a tradition of interpretation that has deep roots but comes to the surface in the twentieth century through such scholars as Ferdinand Weber, Emil Schürer, Wilhelm Bousset, and Rudolf Bultmann.[7] The fundamental ideas inherent in this tradition of Christian scholarship are stated in Sanders's comments on Weber (I have added the numbers in brackets):

> The principal element is the theory [1] that works *earn* salvation; that one's fate is determined by *weighing* fulfillments against transgressions. Maintaining this view necessarily involves [2] *denying* or getting around in some other way *the grace of God in the election.* . . . A third aspect of Weber's view, which is also tied to the theory of salvation by works, is that of establishment of merit and [3] the possibility of a *transfer of merit* at the final judgment. The fourth element has to do with the attitude supposedly reflected in Rabbinic literature: [4] *uncertainty* of salvation mixed with the self-righteous feeling of accomplishment. This too depends on the view that a man is saved by works. He will either be uncertain that he has done enough or proud of having been so righteous. Besides these main elements of Weber's soteriology, [5] his view that God was *inaccessible* has also been maintained to the present day.[8]

These points represent Sanders's concerns about Christian scholarship, and Sanders tells us in the preface what his intent is: "to destroy the view of Rabbinic Judaism which is still prevalent in much, perhaps most, New Testament scholarship."[9] Sanders named names, including the Reformers,[10] and the named scholars became officially sullied. The implication of Sanders's 1977 work was that scholars could no longer assume the traditional theory that Judaism was pockmarked by works righteousness and that therefore Christianity's fundamental difference was that it was a religion of grace. Every new perspective proponent has chimed in on Sanders's critique of Christian scholarship.

7. It is not possible here to provide details; see Sanders, *Paul and Palestinian Judaism,* 1–12, 33–59.

8. Sanders, *Paul and Palestinian Judaism,* 54.

9. Sanders, *Paul and Palestinian Judaism,* xii.

10. For the task of rescuing the Reformers from stereotypes, in part begun by Sanders and continued by others, now read Stephen J. Chester, *Reading Paul with the Reformers: Reconciling Old and New Perspectives* (Grand Rapids: Eerdmans, 2017).

Renewal

The first principle, then, of the new perspective is a reaction to past Christian scholarship on Judaism, and the second is a renewed understanding of Judaism itself. While Sanders found exceptions, and perhaps minimized them, his theory was that Judaism's language of merit and reward and righteousness and obedience and redemption was framed not by works righteousness but by covenant.[11] Sanders, who has been critiqued for running Judaism through a system of salvation derived more from Christianity than from Judaism, as well as for underplaying nomism and portraying an overly simplistic common Judaism, sets out his case for a renewed understanding of Judaism by examining the textual evidence in detail.[12] He studies the rabbis, the Dead Sea Scrolls, the Apocrypha, and the Pseudepigrapha and concludes with these eight points:

> The "pattern" or "structure" of covenantal nomism is this: (1) God has chosen Israel and (2) given the law. The law implies both (3) God's promise to maintain the election and (4) the requirement to obey. (5) God rewards obedience and punishes transgression. (6) The law provides for means of atonement, and atonement results in (7) maintenance or re-establishment of the covenantal relationship. (8) All those who are maintained in the covenant by obedience, atonement and God's mercy belong to the group which will be saved. An important interpretation of the first and last points is that election and ultimately salvation are considered to be by God's mercy rather than human achievement.[13]

This has become Judaism for much, if not most, of New Testament scholarship. While nuances have been added to this basic sketch by Sanders, fundamentally the new perspective embraces Judaism as having a religious pattern of covenantal nomism. Running like a common thread

---

11. An important study on debt as metaphor that expands on Sanders can be found in Gary A. Anderson, *Sin: A History* (New Haven: Yale University Press, 2009).

12. His notion that the function of a religion is about "*how getting in and staying in are understood*" has been criticized for having a Christian soteriology shaping the very function itself. See Sanders, *Paul and Palestinian Judaism*, 17 (italics his). Sanders has clarified that this expression is his way of conveying a larger sense of salvation than individualistic salvation. See Sanders, *Comparing Judaism and Christianity*, 54.

13. Sanders, *Paul and Palestinian Judaism*, 422. This is fleshed out extensively in Sanders, *Judaism: Practice and Belief.*

through both Wright and Dunn, whatever their differences, is this strong renewal of interest in Judaism *as Judaism*.

Reformulation

New perspective scholarship in general agrees with the reaction and the renewal. Where it does not agree is the reformulation of Pauline theology on the basis of the renewal. Is Sanders a *participant in* or the *preparation for* the new perspective? To my knowledge, Sanders has never used the expression for his work, and neither Dunn nor Wright figures much in his recent book on Paul.[14] I will settle here for Sanders as a bridge figure.

All I am attempting to show in this section is how Dunn and Wright reformulate Paul's own theology on the basis of the renewed understanding of Judaism. The crescendo of these two and divergent voices has created the new perspective. It must be reiterated that the most important element of the new perspective is its reaction to previous voices and its renewed interest in an organic understanding of Judaism itself. Only then can one begin to reformulate Pauline theology. The question is, How is Paul's gospel related to covenantal nomism? One of the most significant lines in all of Sanders's scholarship is "In short, *this is what Paul finds wrong in Judaism: it is not Christianity*."[15] Dunn made a big leap forward in filling in what that claim by Sanders meant. (It should be observed that Sanders's famous line created space also for the apocalyptic approach to Paul.)

Dunn's Contribution

In his *Theology of Paul the Apostle*, Dunn follows many of the main soteriological lines of classic Pauline theology in framing the whole of Romans in the categories of soteriology: (1) God and humankind; (2) humankind under indictment, where he discusses Adam, sin, death, and the law; (3) the gospel of Jesus Christ: gospel, Jesus the man, Christ crucified, the risen Lord, the preexistent one, and until Christ returns; (4) the beginning of salvation: the crucial transition, justification, participation, gift of the

---

14. E. P. Sanders, *Paul: The Apostle's Life, Letters, and Thought* (Minneapolis: Fortress, 2015).

15. Sanders, *Paul: The Apostle's Life*, 552 (italics his).

Spirit, baptism; (5) the process of salvation: eschatological tension, Israel; (6) the church: body of Christ, ministry and authority, Lord's Supper; and (7) the behavior of believers: motivating principles and an exposition of Romans 12–15 and 1 Corinthians 5–10.[16] In the second volume of his mammoth Christianity in the Making series, Dunn treats Paul's gospel in slightly reshaped categories: turning from idols to the living God, Christ crucified, God's raising Jesus from the dead, Jesus as Lord, waiting for God's Son from heaven, belief in Christ Jesus, receiving the Holy Spirit, the dinner of the Lord, and the Christian life.[17] In categories there is nothing "new" here.

Dunn's signal contribution to the new perspective reformulation, however, was to propose that "works of the law" did not mean what it meant in pre-Sanders scholarship.[18] Instead of referring to earning merit before God, a category shaped by how pre-Sanders scholars understood Judaism itself, "works of the law" referred, in the first instance, to works required by the law and, in its usage in Galatians and Romans, more particularly and socially to boundary-creating categories like Sabbath, food laws, and circumcision. As Dunn has said it in other places, the law in the context of Galatians and Romans is not about achievement but about *privilege*, Jewish privilege (Rom. 2:12–29).[19] The significance was immediate: what Paul opposed was not "Judaizers" but Jewish proselytizers who demanded that gentile converts to Christ embrace these symbolic (of the whole law) boundary markers, therefore demanding in effect that gentiles become Jews. Dunn often speaks of the polemical edge of (his otherwise) Reformed understanding of justification, namely, by calling it "nationalistic righteousness." Paul, then, is especially pressing against those creating a rift in the church: one branch for Jews and one branch for gentiles. This is where preaching Romans begins for the new perspective: the unity of the church and the inclusion of all.

---

16. Dunn, *Theology of Paul the Apostle.*

17. James D. G. Dunn, *Beginning from Jerusalem*, Christianity in the Making 2 (Grand Rapids: Eerdmans, 2009), 572–87.

18. Dunn has a series of articles on this topic; see the reprints in his collection on the new perspective in Dunn, *New Perspective on Paul*, 121–40, 213–26, 339–45, 381–94, 413–28. He offers his own five-point summary on pp. 16–17. He also responds ably and irenically to his critics on pp. 17–97.

19. Barclay shows that Dunn embraces the priority of grace in Judaism but does not sufficiently embrace the incongruity of grace when Paul's Jewish opponents appeal to their ethnic privilege; see Barclay, *Paul and the Gift*, 164–65.

New perspective Pauline theology, then, is about soteriology—all are indicted, all need to be justified, all are justified by faith alone—but a soteriology shaped for a particular crisis: the conviction by some Jewish believers that gentile believers need to move beyond "God-fearer" status to "proselyte" status by embracing the whole torah. The universal indictment becomes specific in this crisis. Dunn contends that this crisis is what "works of the law" is about in particular situations, and it is this contention that caught the eye of the traditionalists. When "works of the law" is severed from a particular understanding of Augustinian anthropology, Lutherans and the Reformed, some of whom have been vociferous and at times mistaken critics of the new perspective, stand in opposition.[20]

Wright's Contribution

The premier illustration of a lack of consensus in the reformulation of Pauline theology in the wake of the reaction to the traditional view of Judaism and its renewed study following Sanders is the presentation of Paul when one compares Dunn and N. T. Wright. I shall offer some major points on Wright's body of work. First, Wright's first blockbuster was *The New Testament and the People of God*, in which he laid covenantal nomism into the bed of story and his special penchant for distinctions between worldview and theology. This is perhaps Wright's major contribution: the reappreciation and reappropriation of the Old Testament *and* Judaism into a narrative.[21]

Second, Wright's earliest work has never been jettisoned, and that work was the framing of the narrative through the categories of covenant, exile, and the end of exile.[22] Despite pushback, Wright's category remains viable

20. D. A. Carson, Peter T. O'Brien, and Mark A. Seifrid, eds., *Justification and Variegated Judaism*, vol. 1, *The Complexities of Second Temple Judaism*, and vol. 2, *The Paradoxes of Paul* (Grand Rapids: Baker Academic, 2001, 2004).

21. The debate today about linear readings and story from the Old Testament into Judaism to Jesus and the apostles, that is, whether we begin with the narrative and move forward or begin with Jesus and work backward, while important, fundamentally misses the reality that it is both all the time. Too much newness becomes some form of supersessionism and too little newness becomes some form of pluralism. Wright and Dunn escape both charges.

22. Wright, *New Testament and the People of God*, 299–301; N. T. Wright, *Jesus and the Victory of God*, Christian Origins and the Question of God 2 (Minneapolis: Fortress,

and organic to the Bible's own expectations and to Jewish hope. His emphasis that Jewish eschatology often concerned the End of Exile vastly surpasses the categories of classic Christian eschatology. In new perspective fashion, his End of Exile theme emphasizes the continuity with Judaism as well as the newness in Pauline eschatology.

Third, in Wright's hand every central Old Testament theme and Judaism's central motifs—such as covenant, law, Spirit, Israel, land—are both reaffirmed and reworked in Paul. Hence, the three main sections of his magisterial *Paul and the Faithfulness of God*: (1) the one God of Israel, *freshly revealed* in Christ; (2) the people of God, *freshly reworked* in the church; and (3) God's future for the world, *freshly imagined* in the new heavens and the new earth under creation's one true Lord, King Jesus. If Wright's narrative bed for covenantal nomism was a signal contribution, in these themes we see the new perspective's continued focus on both continuity and newness.

Fourth, in about 2000 a theme emerged with greater force in Wright's studies of Paul, namely, the empire or, better yet, anti-imperial criticism.[23] This theme, which has been prominent in Wright's work for almost two decades, has undergone shifts; at least I have perceived a lessening of emphasis, but at the same time—yet again—a fresher and solid anchoring of the theme in Judaism's own critique of paganism and empire.[24]

Fifth, Wright's landing spot for Pauline theology's on-the-ground reality is nothing less than the preacher's platform: reconciliation. Wright's redemptive, ecclesial, creational reality for the believer is this: God has reconciled all things in Christ; the believer is reconciled in Christ; believers are reconciled with one another; the Christian is an agent of reconciliation in the world; the kingdom is new creation fully reconciled.[25]

It is right at this point that I believe the new perspective acquires force:

- If Judaism is characterized as covenantal nomism,
- if the Christian faith is the fulfillment of the Old Testament,
- if God is revealed in Christ,

1996); Wright, *Paul and the Faithfulness of God*; James M. Scott, ed., *Exile: A Conversation with N. T. Wright* (Downers Grove, IL: IVP Academic, 2017).

23. Wright, *Pauline Perspectives*, esp. 169–90, 223–36, 237–54, 317–31, 439–51; Wright, *Paul and the Faithfulness of God*.

24. Wright, *Paul and the Faithfulness of God*, 279–347, 1271–319.

25. See Wright, *Paul and the Faithfulness of God*, 1487–516. Wright's some thirty pages deserve fuller treatment than I can provide here.

- if justification is by faith alone but also the inclusion of gentiles by faith,
- if Israel is expanded to include gentiles in the church,
- if eschatology is reworked into kingdom theology by Jesus and the apostle,
- *then* gentiles-in-the-church-as-reworked-Israel is the on-the-ground-redemptive-reality for Pauline theology.

The church thus becomes the agent and location of reconciliation in the world, and this raises the significance of Romans, specifically the Weak and the Strong of Romans 14–15, to the top of Pauline theology.

My purpose here is to sketch one person's suggestions on how to preach Romans in the new perspective framework, but one more matter needs mention: Dunn and Wright, especially in their earlier forays into reformulating Pauline theology as a result of Sanders's covenantal nomism, made some bold claims and strong denials of traditional theology that neither helped their agendas nor made friends of traditional readers of Paul. Time has worn the edges off most of these sharper claims, and moderating positions have been achieved in most cases.

Romans after the Reformulation(s)

At this point I could continue with a description of how Dunn and Wright read Romans, but instead of doing that I propose to sketch in more general terms how the new perspective—and I consider myself a proponent—understands Romans. In this sketch, then, the reader will hear as much a synthesis of Dunn and Wright as McKnight.[26]

Romans 12–16: Others, Love, Peace, Spirit

First, to preach Romans well one must begin at the end. Until the context of Romans (at least the context of Romans that Paul made evident in this letter) is clear, one cannot begin well. It is of course true that the letter works from 1:1 on and not from 16:27 backward, but what we need before us are the concrete situations at work in Rome that percolate constantly in 12:1–16:27 and bubble over in 1:1–11:36. Once we become familiar with

---

26. See Dunn, *Romans*; Wright, "Letter to the Romans."

the issues in the final chapters, we notice them in the earlier chapters. The fundamental elements of this context include the Weak and the Strong, the relations of the Christians of Rome with the state, the collection for the poor saints in Jerusalem, the mission of Paul to Spain, and the way the Christians are to live with one another in this swirl of issues—all in what looks like five or six house churches.[27]

The Weak are Jewish believers and the Strong gentile believers, though rigid classification by ethnicity or religion would be a mistake. Furthermore, there are good reasons to think Strong and Weak are deeply social status categories: the Strong are the Powerful and the Weak are the Disempowered.[28] The Jew Paul in 15:1 lines himself up with the Strong when he says, "We who are strong."[29] The Strong, then, is not a simple code word but instead expresses those who are predominantly gentile who know that the torah is not demanded of them, which means the Weak are Jewish believers who for one reason or another think the torah in various halakic forms needs to be observed by all.[30] Paul has strong words for the Strong: the gentile believers of Rome are running roughshod over the sensitivities and sensibilities of the Jewish believers. This is nothing less than a reversal of angles found in Galatians, where some were pressing the gentile wing into conformity with the torah. Pressure by Paul especially on the Strong becomes important in our reading of Romans.

Many have read Romans 13:1–7 in a conservative manner and have diminished the command to submit to government in a variety of contextualizing ways: some think Paul seeks to contain enthusiastic revolutionaries, others think that Paul is pastorally comforting those stressed by Rome's treatment of Jews and Christians, and others see here a local disturbance of the increased pressure of taxation—all giving an "out" on the permanence of governmental authority.[31] Some think it is Paul at his pragmatic or missional best. Others find hints—not least in beginning the section at 12:21,

27. Regarding the first element, see Mark Reasoner, *The Strong and the Weak: Romans 14.1–15.13 in Context*, Society for New Testament Studies Monograph Series 103 (Cambridge: Cambridge University Press, 1999).

28. I am persuaded that the Strong-Weak tension runs throughout the entire letter. For previous scholarship for this approach, see P. S. Minear, *The Obedience of Faith: The Purposes of Paul in the Epistle to the Romans*, Studies in Biblical Theology 2.19 (London: SCM, 1971); A. J. M. Wedderburn, *The Reasons for Romans* (Minneapolis: Fortress, 1991).

29. Scripture quotations are from the NRSV.

30. While some think Strong and Weak is current jargon at Rome, the presence of the same terms in 1 Cor. 8–10 for different issues suggests this is Pauline language.

31. See Mark Reasoner, *Romans in Full Circle: A History of Interpretation* (Louisville: Westminster John Knox, 2005), 129–42.

or harking back to 12:9's theme of love or 12:19's curbing of vengeance—of a serious diminishment of the submission to the powers (13:1). The lack of interpretive consensus frustrates, but it is at least reasonable to think the Christians of Rome were concerned about Rome's imperial forces—a concern characteristic of Christians throughout the world today and therefore a concern for preaching Romans well. There are good reasons to think the target audience of Romans 13:1–7 is the Weak who are tempted to resist paying taxes on the basis of a Jewish tradition of zealotry.

At work in Paul's mission, whether one sees the extension of the collection throughout his entire ministry or two collections (one early, one late), is Paul's summons to his gentile churches to offer monetary support for the poor saints of Jerusalem. This collection for the saints is at the heart of his Aegean mission (Gal. 2:10; 1 Cor. 16:1–4; 2 Cor. 8–9; Rom. 15:16, 25–28, 30–32; cf. Acts 11:30; 12:25; 24:17).[32] This issue, presented in Romans 15 in clearly liturgical and cultic terms, emerges to press home to the Roman Christians that they may be at the center of the empire but the center of God's work remains Jerusalem. A complement to decentering Rome is Paul's planned mission to Spain (15:24), a theme given special prominence by Robert Jewett, and also brings to the fore the international connectedness of the churches.[33] Jew and gentile are brought into one new household of faith in Christ by the power of the Spirit.

Paul is a pastor thinking of local house churches where the Strong are to open the doors and welcome (to the table) the Weak, and thereby create a fellowship of siblings.[34] His principal themes for the Christian life in this last section of Romans, then, are

- the sacrifice of one's entire person to God in personal transformation (12:1–2);
- love manifesting itself in many ways, including a powerful vision of mutual regard for the conscience and decisions of others (12:9, 19; 13:8–9, 10; 14:15; 15:30; 16:5, 8–9, 12); and
- peace, unity, and tolerance (12:16; 14:17, 19; 15:13, 33; 16:20).

32. See Stephan Joubert, *Paul as Benefactor: Reciprocity, Strategy and Theological Reflection in Paul's Collection*, WUNT 2.124 (Tübingen: Mohr Siebeck, 2000); Bruce W. Longenecker, *Remember the Poor: Paul, Poverty, and the Greco-Roman World* (Grand Rapids: Eerdmans, 2010); David J. Downs, *The Offering of the Gentiles: Paul's Collection for Jerusalem in Its Chronological, Cultural, and Cultic Contexts* (Grand Rapids: Eerdmans, 2016).

33. Robert Jewett, *Romans: A Commentary*, Hermeneia (Minneapolis: Fortress, 2006).

34. I find Jewett's sketch compelling even though I'm not as convinced as he is of the tenement nature of the house churches; see Jewett, *Romans*, 952–53.

While these virtues cannot be reduced only to the Strong-Weak issue, they are tailored explicitly for that situation at Rome. None of this happens apart from the grace of God in Christ who *through the Spirit* is transforming the Strong and the Weak into siblings (12:11; 14:17; 15:13, 16, 19, 30).

Romans 9–11: God's Covenant Faithfulness Includes Gentiles

To preach Romans one must also know Paul's story, and we are fortunate to have so much of that story put on display in Romans 9–11, a three-chapter section sometimes (mis)considered as a parenthesis in Paul's letter. Not so, for it tells us how Paul read his Bible, where he located the Roman Empire, and how that story related to the Strong-Weak divide in the Roman house churches.[35] Let us recall that Paul's big concern is pressure on the Weak by the Strong, the supposed liberated high status party of gentile believers who look down—a very Roman thing to do—on those they consider Weak, namely, Jewish believers with a continuing commitment to some forms of torah observance. When I read and preach Romans, I do my best to keep this vision in mind: the Strong are pressuring the Weak, and Paul is pressing the Strong to dwell in peace and love with the Weak in a way that treats them as siblings, all the while raising up the importance of mutual respect for one another's decisions. The theme of the Strong and Weak runs right through the entire Letter to the Romans, but I will indicate in this chapter only a few traces of that theme and leave to a longer treatment a fuller display.

Pauline ethics, if I may reduce it for the moment to Romans 12–16, is propped up by a narrative that runs through Paul's mind as he attempts to explain his gospel to house churches that mostly don't know him, as he solicits support for his Spanish mission, and as he seeks pastorally to persuade the Strong to treat the Weak as siblings and the Weak to comprehend the freshness of Christian ethics. This narrative, however, is not Paul's narrative but Paul's perception of God's own surprising moves and plan for history as revealed in Israel's story. One quick glance at standard printed Bibles today (I have the NRSV in front of me alongside the Greek New Testament) shows Paul's quotation of poetic lines from the Old Testament. (Echoes have to be discerned by the trained reader.)[36]

---

35. Bruce W. Longenecker, ed., *Narrative Dynamics in Paul: A Critical Assessment* (Louisville: Westminster John Knox, 2002).

36. Richard B. Hays, *The Faith of Jesus Christ: The Narrative Substructure of Galatians*

Richard Hays pulls together various elements of Paul's/Israel's narrative at work in Romans 9–11, focusing on the intertextuality of Isaiah's prophecies and articulating how these citations and echoes are woven into Paul's narrative web of Israel's story.[37] But these elements emerge from an existing narrative of covenant election of Israel, Israel's calling in the world, the giving of the torah as a way of life for the covenant people (covenantal nomism), the ups and downs of Israel's history, and most decisively—apocalyptically!—for Paul, the arrival of the Messiah as God's redemptive agent who puts exile into the past. Knowing Christ as God's Messiah allows Paul to rework Israel's history toward and from Christ. That foundation gives rise to the problem that Israel has not believed but gentiles have; Paul's mission is more successful with gentiles than Jews, *but Paul knows in the depth of his heart that God's covenant faithfulness will not be averted by Jewish rejection.* Israel remains God's people, even if now expanded and expanding to include gentiles.

The narrative of Paul that we must keep in mind when preaching Romans is that *God remains faithful to the covenant, redemption is entirely God's act, and God's faithfulness entails inclusion of gentiles.* Thus, we read in Romans 9:6 the pondering of Paul that "it is not as though the word of God had failed," and at 11:1 this: "I ask, then, has God rejected his people? By no means!" How does Paul know? His own story tells him so: "I myself am an Israelite, a descendant of Abraham, a member of the tribe of Benjamin." The rejection of the Messiah by Jews and the acceptance by gentiles, then, do not put into question the covenant faithfulness of God to Israel. After all, "they are Israelites, and to them belong the adoption, the glory, the covenants, the giving of the law, the worship, and the promises; to them belong the patriarchs, and from them, according to the flesh, comes the Messiah, who is over all, God blessed forever. Amen" (9:4–5).

To be sure, there is an elect within the elect: those who are children of the promise are true Israelites (9:6–8). God's mercy creates what might be called "the promise line of people" who stand over against the hardening and wrath of others (9:18), but the issue cannot be reduced to the inscrutability of God, because it is simultaneously an issue of faith (9:32). And this permits Paul to bring in, as he did in Galatians 3:15–4:7, where the law fits.

3:1–4:11, 2nd ed. (Grand Rapids: Eerdmans, 2002); Hays, *Echoes of Scripture in the Letters of Paul* (New Haven: Yale University Press, 1993); Hays, *The Conversion of the Imagination: Paul as Interpreter of Israel's Scripture* (Grand Rapids: Eerdmans, 2005).

37. Hays, *Conversion of the Imagination*, 45–47.

In Romans the law has reached its telos in Christ (10:4). Why? So the privilege of Israel's role may be expanded to include all who believe (10:4). Paul poses "doing" against "believing," not because he thinks believing doesn't include works, but because one is about the boundary markers created by law (privilege of the Weak) and the other about including gentiles (10:5–21).

All of these back-and-forths lead Paul directly to theology, that is, to God's covenant faithfulness to Israel in spite of unbelief. In fact, the unbelief leads to gentile belief (11:11–12) *as well as a harvest for Israelites too* (11:12). A sudden move to the gentiles reveals what's uppermost on Paul's mind: the Strong and the Weak. In fact, Romans 9:1–11:10 focuses on the Weak while 11:11–36 is more concerned with the Strong. Hence, gentile believers are not to repeat Israel's unbelief or they, like unbelieving Israelites, will also be cut off (11:17–24). After all, Israel is the "root that supports you" (11:18). The mystery for Paul is the temporary hardening of Israel through its unbelief, but the hope for Paul is that "all Israel will be saved" (11:26). We are back to the theme of these chapters: God is faithful to his covenant with Israel, but that faithfulness needs to be matched by faithfulness on the part of both Israelites and gentiles.

Which means the Strong are not privileged; they are no different than individual Israelites in God's election of Israel—which means the Strong too must be faithful or they can be cut out. Noticeably in Romans, faithfulness for the Strong means embracing the Weak. Romans 9–11, then, needs to shove away from the old comfortable shoreline where one could talk in terms of predestination, calling, regeneration, and other elements in the *ordo salutis* for individuals—and worry about whether one is in or out. Rather, the fundamental themes of these chapters are about God's faithfulness to God's covenant with Israel when Israel is not responding to its Messiah and gentiles are. These chapters, focused as they seemingly are until 11:10 on the Weak, are a pastoral narrative put to use to exhort the Christians of Rome to unity. Which means preaching these chapters is fundamentally a task of preaching the expansion of the people of God to include those seemingly excluded, which in my context in Chicagoland means a very sharp rebuke to racism and ethnic silos systemically created to cause white flight, protect suburban wealth, and manage urban ghettos—conditions all mimicked in segregated churches. In Romans, especially 9–11, privilege is dealt the cold hand of judgment: the Weak are not to sit in judgment, and the Strong are not to claim superiority. It's all God's grace and God's mercy, and that grace is for all. Those who know God's grace are siblings, not rivals.

But Romans 9–11 makes sense only because of the indictment of Romans 1:18–2:29 (and beyond) and the wider themes of Romans 1–8, and many now observe that Romans 9–11 resolves the problem at work in Romans 1–8.

Finally, Romans 1–8: Jews and Gentiles, Redemption, Spirit

That context (Rom. 12–16) and that narrative (Rom. 9–11), I contend, lie behind all the theology of the gospel and redemption at work in Romans 1–8. The gospel's thematic statements are by most accounts to be found in 1:1–6 and 1:16–17:

> Paul, a servant of Jesus Christ, called to be an apostle, set apart for the gospel of God, which he promised beforehand through his prophets in the holy scriptures, the gospel concerning his Son, who was descended from David according to the flesh and was declared to be Son of God with power according to the spirit of holiness by resurrection from the dead, Jesus Christ our Lord, through whom we have received grace and apostleship to bring about the obedience of faith among all the Gentiles for the sake of his name, including yourselves who are called to belong to Jesus Christ. (1:1–6)

> For I am not ashamed of the gospel; it is the power of God for salvation to everyone who has faith, to the Jew first and also to the Greek. For in it the righteousness of God is revealed through faith for faith; as it is written, "The one who is righteous will live by faith." (1:16–17)

Already the Strong and Weak are echoed in the focus on Israel's Scriptures and the descent from David, in "among all the Gentiles for the sake of his name," and most especially in "to the Jew first and also to the Greek." That is, Paul presses his case immediately: the Strong are not superior; Israel has a covenant priority to the gentiles; but the gospel incorporates the gentile believer into the one people of God, Jew or gentile. Those included are there by God's grace through faith.

Paul is not as focused on personal salvation, according to most readings of Romans, as he is on demonstrating that gentiles are sinners and thus the Strong are leveled (1:18–32), but this is not an either-or: all are in need of personal redemption, and the Weak will perhaps find some delight in these lines in Romans. A more careful reading of Romans 1:18–32, when tied close to chapter two, reveals that 1:18–32 is a rhetorical set-up. That is, these verses are a stereotype of gentile pagan idolaters, echoing the Wisdom of Solomon. The Weak are in mind: they sit in judgment on the pagans of Rome and Paul gives with one hand and then takes back with the other in chapter two. The stereotype is turned against the Weak in Romans 2. The Weak have no final claim on God's grace and are themselves not to sit in judgment on others (2:1–3:8). Everyone—gentile and Jew, Strong and Weak—is undone (3:9–20), but both the Strong and the Weak are redeemed—justified by faith—by Christ.

Many read Romans so soteriologically that the climax of the book is Romans 3:21–26, but a close reading of Romans 3 shows that 3:19–20's statement is "glossed" by 3:21–26, resuming Paul's remonstration with the Weak of Rome in 3:27–4:25. Paul continues to answer typical questions posed by the Weak that began in Romans 2 and continue through Romans 4. What is sometimes missed in 3:21–31 is Paul's emphasis on gentile integration into the one people of God, words clearly aimed at the Weak (3:27–31). While personal salvation is entailed in what Paul is saying, his focus is also on ecclesial expansion—that is, on the inclusion of Jews and gentiles in the one family of God, on the basis of Christ's crucifixion and resurrection, through faith alone and not by works (the Mosaic law expressed by faithful boundary-marking practices that would separate the Weak and the Strong). Jimmy Dunn's emphasis that justification is by faith alone *but also* about the inclusion of gentiles in the one family of God is spot on. That is clearly Paul's emphasis when justification is the subject.

At the heart of Paul's concern with the Weak and Strong is that the Weak want torah (halakically lived) while the Strong want no part of that. Paul's polemic about (1) the works of the law and (2) Abraham as an exemplum of faith are both theoretical (personal justification is by faith alone, not by works) and contextually aimed (justification concerns including gentiles in the one family of God). That is, "works of the law" is both an anthropological problem and a covenant faithfulness and boundary marker problem. To the Weak, Paul says Abraham was justified not by works but by faith (4:1–5:12; for preaching Romans, one needs constantly to keep in mind and reread the simpler Gal. 3:19–4:7).[38] Thus, to the Weak he offers the reminder that Abraham has "descendants" among the gentiles (4:16). One

---

38. See the fascinating essay "Paul and the Patriarch: The Role(s) of Abraham in Galatians and Romans," in Wright, *Pauline Perspectives*, 554–92.

has to wonder if Romans 1–4 is aimed at the Weak while Romans 5–8 is aimed at the Strong, and if Romans 5–8 is the gospel of and for the Strong.

In reading Romans I suggest that if we begin with the context in Romans 12–16 and let those categories shape our reading of the rest of the letter we see that Romans 5–8 is the solution to the Strong-Weak divide: the solution is not torah observance nor reckless freedom but life in the Spirit. But Romans 1–8 is not abstract theology that is then applied in Romans 12–16 but the reverse: Romans 12–16 is the "lived theology" that is propped up by the more abstract theology of both Romans 1–8 and 9–11. The people of God can be transformed into a unity only if they learn life in the Spirit.

This Israel-transformative redemption in Christ is prompted by the gracious love of God (5:8) while it is also generated by the Spirit (5:5). The Jew and gentile theme for most readings of Romans comes to its climax in Romans 5:12–21, where Paul moves behind Abraham to Adam and fashions famous theological expressions that become the foundation of so much of the Western theological tradition. His polar opposites still preach, but they were vital for the Strong-Weak divide in Rome:

Adam: sin, condemnation, death
Christ: obedience, justification, eternal life

Preaching Romans then means preaching the consequences of sin and redemption in Christ alone for each person listening. Behind and inside the Abrahamic covenant is the Adamic condition.[39]

This focus on everyone being a sinner, which for many begins at 1:18 and emerges with force once again in 5:12–21, creates a problem that seems as much focused on the Strong as it is on the Weak. The Strong because they sense that liberation might be an opportunity for grace and forgiveness; the Weak because they fear that righteousness and holiness may be diminished. Paul tackles both, one in each arm, in chapter 6: everyone—Weak and Strong—who believes is baptized into both Christ's death and his resurrection. Which means they have all died to sin and are now all raised to a life of righteousness. We see here the commonly needed pastoral sensitivity to two (or more!) parties in the church at the same time. The Strong are told

---

39. No one preaching Rom. 5:12–21 today can avoid the issue of the historical Adam or the problem of evolutionary creation and faith; see Dennis R. Venema and Scot McKnight, *Adam and the Genome: Reading Scripture after Genetic Science* (Grand Rapids: Brazos, 2017).

that their baptism means liberation from sin into righteousness, and the Weak are told that their baptism leads to righteousness as well, but with an added twist: this is not accomplished by the law (6:14).[40]

A comprehensive discussion of Romans 7 would illustrate the various approaches in this volume, but there is not space here for that discussion.[41] The question for us here is "Who is this Ego?" when Paul writes thus:

> If it had not been for the law, I would not have known sin. I would not have known what it is to covet if the law had not said, "You shall not covet." But sin, seizing an opportunity in the commandment, produced in me all kinds of covetousness. Apart from the law sin lies dead. I was once alive apart from the law, but when the commandment came, sin revived and I died, and the very commandment that promised life proved to be death to me. For sin, seizing an opportunity in the commandment, deceived me and through it killed me. (7:7–11)

If a traditional reading is the anthropological lens of Augustine, where the person in God's grace nevertheless struggles with merit, sin, and obedience, the new perspective focuses on Romans 7 as an apology for the law, life in the Spirit, and grace and on the shift in eschatological ages from Adam to Christ.[42] N. T. Wright presses his narrative approach to find a solution to Romans 7: the Ego is Israel, specifically Israel's story under the law (hence, we are back to Gal. 3:19–4:7 again) and its calling to observe torah and at the same time discover its punishing powers.[43] Israel's solution is found in Romans 8:3–4: Christ, Spirit, empowerment *to do God's law*. The Weak, I add, are encouraged to be torah obedient, again with a twist: through the Spirit who generates, as in Romans 12–16, other-orientation, love, and peace. Simultaneously, the Strong are warned that Spirit-prompted living is consistent with torah. Thus, Romans 7:5–6 will be the center of preaching Romans 7: "While we were living in the flesh, our sinful passions, aroused by the law, were at work in our members to bear fruit for death. But now we are discharged from the law, dead to that

---

40. Readers of Romans need to pay attention to personal pronouns: first person (I and we), second person (you), and third person (it, she, he, they). I cannot address this issue in this chapter.

41. Begin with Reasoner, *Romans in Full Circle*, 67–84.

42. See esp. Reasoner, *Romans in Full Circle*, 81.

43. Wright, "Romans," 549–57.

which held us captive, so that we are slaves not under the old written code but in the new life of the Spirit."

If one wants reduced language: Paul finds the entire solution to Israel's history in a Christocentric pneumatology or a pneumatic Christology. That is, the central preaching text for Romans 8 is verses 3–4: "For God has done what the law, weakened by the flesh, could not do: by sending his own Son in the likeness of sinful flesh, and to deal with sin, he condemned sin in the flesh, so that the just requirement of the law might be fulfilled in us, who walk not according to the flesh but according to the Spirit."

We have now come full circle: the Weak and the Strong are summoned to baptism, which means death to sin (superiorities and judgmentalisms) and raised to new life (other-orientation, love, peace). They are summoned even deeper in the waters to the new creation God has established in Christ and the Spirit, and life in the Spirit simply doesn't look like how the Roman churches are behaving right now. But if they hear Paul out and embrace the gospel of God's grace in Christ through the Spirit, they will create a "fellowship of differents" that transcends Roman imperial ideologies.[44] If that doesn't preach, nothing does.

---

44. The title of my popular book on the Christian life in Paul: Scot McKnight, *A Fellowship of Differents: Showing the World God's Design for Life Together* (Grand Rapids: Zondervan, 2015).

3

Romans and the Apocalyptic Reading of Paul

Douglas A. Campbell

The antecedents of the apocalyptic reading of Paul stretch back to key German scholars working on the New Testament at the dawn of the twentieth century.[1] But we have not been able to speak, until relatively recently, of a group or party that constitutes a significant ongoing presence within Paul's scholarly discussion, especially in North America.[2] Yet we can do so now, and there is one principal reason for this: J. Louis (Lou) Martyn (1925–2015). Martyn, through his meticulously insightful work, especially, but not exclusively, on Galatians, and through his recruitment of a network of friends and protégés, has generated a powerful reading of Paul's gospel that representatives of both old and new perspectives are right to be threatened by. Martyn's work now anchors Paul's apocalyptic construal.

Revelation versus Foundationalism

Martyn is important first of all because he affirms how Paul's gospel declaration rests on a revelation from God centered on Jesus. Martyn makes this claim in one of his earliest essays, published in 1967, and reiterates it in his magisterial Galatians commentary, published in 1997.[3] The resulting reading of Paul is usefully known as "apocalyptic" because the Greek for "revelation," which Paul uses in Galatians 1:12 and elsewhere, is *apokalyp-*

---

1. Esp. William Wrede, Albert Schweitzer, and Ernst Käsemann.

2. Any list of contemporary Pauline interpreters who advocate Martyn's basic approach to Paul should include Martin de Boer, Alexandra Brown, Charlie Cousar, Susan Eastman, Beverly Gaventa, Katherine Grieb, Douglas Harink, Leander Keck, and me.

3. J. Louis Martyn, *Galatians* (New York: Doubleday, 1997). See also his essay collection, *Theological Issues in the Letters of Paul* (Edinburgh: T&T Clark, 1997). "Epistemology at the Turn of the Ages: 2 Corinthians 5.16," first published in 1967, can be accessed most easily in *Theological Issues*, 89–110.

sis.[4] It is critical to appreciate that this is a claim about *epistemology* or truth criteria, as the title to his 1967 essay indicates, "Epistemology at the Turn of the Ages."

Epistemology raises a vital issue. Many of us frequently make various claims about what God is like and is doing as we expound the Bible, develop our theology, and preach and teach. But how do we know that what we are saying about God is true? This pressing question leads us to consider our truth criteria, this being the concern of epistemology. What criteria are we using to judge the truth or falsity of our statements? How are we measuring the accuracy of our God talk? Obviously a great deal rests on this—nothing less than whether we are speaking the truth about God or are lost in our own illusions—and at this moment it will prove helpful to take a short detour from Martyn to Karl Barth, to further clarify what is at stake.

Some time ago, Barth inaugurated a theological recovery of the Bible's approach to truth criteria over against the ostensibly sophisticated approach to truth of the modern university, which had led, in his experience, to complicity by his learned divinity professors in the inauguration of two world wars. Barth saw with prophetic clarity that modernity had been led astray by believing that the establishment of the truth or falsity of statements about God rested ultimately in the hands of humanity, who developed their most basic truth criteria for themselves and then judged statements about God to be true or false in their light. This was well-intentioned (and it wasn't just a modern phenomenon).[5] Moreover, it could even look quite theological. Truth criteria could be derived by contemplating nature as God's creation, or by looking deep within human consciousness and describing the human spirit (and so on). The key problem, however, was that God's activity in Jesus was being judged by these prior criteria instead of these criteria being brought themselves under the judgment of God as revealed by Jesus. If Jesus was the revelation of God, as the creeds have always affirmed, then he has to be our key truth criterion and there can be no other; in that case we would be admitting other lords beside and even above *the* Lord. Jesus's truth must be lord over and judge all other truths. Crucially, this means that the truth about the overriding, sovereign truth that is Jesus *is internal to its arrival.* We learn when this truth arrives that it is self-authenticating. In more bib-

---

4. See, e.g., Ernst Käsemann's exposition of Rom. 1:17 in his *Commentary on Romans,* 4th ed., trans. Geoffrey W. Bromiley (Grand Rapids: Eerdmans, 1980), esp. 30.

5. Michael J. Buckley, *At the Origins of Modern Atheism* (New Haven: Yale University Press, 1987).

lical parlance, it is an *apokalypsis* or revelation. God reveals the truth about God as that truth is definitively disclosed by Jesus.

Barth had no trouble finding a lot of evidence for this in the Bible, as did Martyn more narrowly within Paul. (Note that the Bible attests to this truth; it does not establish it.) Anyone reading Galatians will notice that Paul speaks at length in his opening argument about the way God's revelation in Jesus smashed into his zealously misdirected life and completely reoriented it. Paul, Barth, and Martyn are consequently all on the same page here, as am I. We know about God definitively because of Jesus, and we know about him because God has revealed him to us (so 1 Cor. 2:1–10), at which moment we need to talk about the Spirit as well. The triune God reveals the triune God, although chosen human representatives like Paul are involved as well, *mediating* this revelation to anyone who will listen to it.[6]

But there is a sinister flip side to this insight. Barth also saw with great clarity what happens when people insist on asking if the truth that is Jesus's revelation of God is itself true, evaluating this truth with some other truth criteria that they have developed for themselves and that are then placed over the top of the truth that is God. This process is usefully known as "theological foundationalism," because people thereby construct their own foundations for evaluating God and God's truth (see 1 Cor. 3:10–15). The damage resulting from this hubris became particularly clear to Barth in Europe during the 1930s, when the vast majority of the German church, then the most sophisticated Christian nation in the world, cooperated enthusiastically with the rise to power of National Socialism, compounding its earlier compromises with aggressive German expansion in World War I.[7] Barth articulated his insights sharply in a famous exchange with Emil Brunner in 1934, who had affirmed the possibility of deriving knowledge about God from the spirit of a nation's history and culture, independently of a direct relationship with Jesus Christ—in retrospect, a disastrous thing to affirm in Europe in the 1930s.[8] Barth's charge against Brunner was that

6. See my tentatively titled *Pauline Dogmatics in Outline: From Revelation to Race* (Grand Rapid: Eerdmans, forthcoming), chap. 3, "A God of Love," elaborating texts such as Rom. 1:1–6, 8–15; 15:15–21.

7. See Eberhard Busch, *Karl Barth: His Life from Letters and Autobiographical Texts*, 2nd rev. ed., trans. J. Bowden (London: SCM, 1976), 216–53.

8. "No!," in *Natural Theology*, trans. Peter Fraenkel (Eugene, OR: Wipf & Stock, 2002), 67–128. It was echoed in the Barmen Declaration, which was written by Barth, and in volume 1 of the *Church Dogmatics*, ed. T. F. Torrance and G. W. Bromiley, 4 vols. in 13 parts (Edinburgh: T&T Clark, 1956–1996 [1932–1967]).

when the starting point for Christian truth that is the revelation of God in Jesus Christ is abandoned, the church loses its way. It becomes incapable of distinguishing between God's commands and commands arising from its own culture, and evil exploits this confusion, resulting in complicity in oppression and violence. The Bible relates this awful spiral to "idolatry," and instructs in counterpoint that God must not be imaged, which is really just to say that God is in charge of what God looks like (Exod. 20:2–6; Deut. 5:6–10).

In view of all this, Martyn's sustained emphasis on the epistemology of revelation in Paul could hardly be more important, and this has to be the first key element in Paul's apocalyptic construal. It is the *sine qua non* of further insight. Without it we immediately lose our way, along with any possibility of adjudicating competing claims made by other Christians about God and God's claims on us.[9]

Apocalyptic Storytelling

Now that we have realized that Jesus is the definitive truth concerning God as revealed by God, we need to attend closely to the content of this revelation. What does Jesus reveal? It will be hard to go much further without telling a story, and it is critical that this story is told in a certain apocalyptic way.

Stories are our way of describing people—how they act through time, what they intend, how they interrelate, and hence what they are like as people. Moreover, as Jesus reveals, God is personal in a way that exceeds most of our categories for even saying this. Paul constantly calls his converts to respond to God the Father, to his Son, our Lord, and to the Holy Spirit, who is also the Spirit of Jesus. So we now need to tell a story.[10] But we must avoid falling into the same trap we just detailed as we tell it.

Stories often have a problem-solution structure and consequently work forward. They set up a difficulty, and then usually (although not invariably) the story's heroic protagonist overcomes it. (Think of all the superhero

9. See esp. Alan J. Torrance, "*Auditus Fidei*: Where and How Does God Speak? Faith, Reason, and the Question of Criteria," in *Reason and the Reasons of Faith*, ed. Paul J. Griffiths and Reinhardt Hütter (New York: T&T Clark International, 2005), 27–52.

10. See Stanley Hauerwas, *The Peaceable Kingdom: A Primer in Christian Ethics* (Notre Dame, IN: University of Notre Dame Press, 1983).

stories so beloved of the American public.)[11] But Jesus is our definitive truth, so there is a sense in which we cannot know the problem before he, as the solution, arrives. We cannot tell the apocalyptic story forward, and trying to do so will betray it.

To know a problem in detail is always to know the solution already. Our problem might be a flat tire on our car. In this case, we know that the solution is to get the punctured tire patched at a garage, and then to get the doughnut tire off and the repaired tire back on. To know the problem *is* to know the solution, and when the solution arrives—the repaired tire—it adds nothing to our knowledge of the situation. When we tell this story forward, all the key information arrives with the problem, which is the punctured tire.

But if we tell the story of Jesus in this way, with some detailed account of our problem, we define why he is coming before he arrives and thereby take control over his truth. Our account of the problem, developed before his arrival, will dictate who he is and what he does. Hence our account of the problem will be our ultimate truth, and Jesus will arrive like a repaired tire and be fitted onto a problem that we have already worked out for ourselves—an instance of theological foundationalism, albeit undertaken with the best of intentions. Rather, if Jesus is the definitive truth, he will have to tell us why he has come. If we have a problem, he will have to tell us what this is after he has arrived. So the apocalyptic story will have to work *backward* or *retrospectively*. In the light of Jesus's arrival, we will see what our situation is really like. Insofar as we have a problem, his definitive solution will tell us what our problem is. So the story of God acting through Jesus must unfold like a memoir, a story that looks back on a life and reflects on its significance with hindsight, finding a meaning and direction only apparent with that hindsight.[12]

Deliverance

Looking back on our past situation through the lens of Jesus's great battle with evil in the cross and resurrection, we do see that we have a problem;

11. See Robert Jewett, *The Captain America Complex: The Dilemma of Zealous Nationalism* (Santa Fe: Bear & Company, 1984 [orig. 1973]).

12. See, e.g., Stanley Hauerwas, *Hannah's Child: A Theologian's Memoir* (Grand Rapids: Eerdmans, 2012).

indeed, we see a human plight that is piteous (Rom. 7:24). But, crucially, this is now revealed to be, as Martyn said, a "four-actor," not a "three-actor," drama.[13] We learn this because Jesus *liberates* us from something. Jesus's salvation is a deliverance from the incarcerating state Paul calls the flesh. The flesh sins, but not simply of its own volition. It is deceived (7:7–13) and enslaved (7:14–25) by something Paul dramatizes as "Sin" in Romans 5–7 but describes elsewhere in terms of lustful passions. The location of these lusts in our very being (5:12) has introduced an ongoing propensity to sin and the inevitable consequence of this: a long spiral through corruption into death. And to make matters worse, we are beset from without by evil powers under the leadership of Satan (8:38–39). So the state of the flesh is indeed piteous. Consequently, Jesus's liberation of us from the flesh, as he lifts us into a new, resurrected, and spiritual state, discloses a radical account of our current problematic situation that Paul narrates in terms of Adam. The flesh cannot simply be repaired or healed. It must be *terminated* and *reconstituted*.

Several critical features of this salvation should be noted:

1. Both the cross *and* the resurrection play saving roles for Paul. Jesus terminates our corrupted condition on the cross and sets us free into a new life through the resurrection (and the divine Spirit is at work here as well: 8:1–14). Paul interprets the entry ritual of baptism in Romans 6 as enacting our death, burial, and resurrection in Jesus, whereby we enter in some sense into Jesus's present resurrected and ascended state now. A saving emphasis on the resurrection is consequently a hallmark of the apocalyptic reading of Paul, probably because it was a hallmark of Paul's. "He was delivered [up to death] for our transgressions, and *raised to life for our deliverance* [*dikaiōsis*]" (4:25).[14]

2. The Jewish Apocalypses now enter the picture in an appropriate way. We do not need to limit the historical background sources for Paul's thinking to these texts, as some opine, but insofar as the Apocalypses speak of resurrection and cosmic transformation as God's solution to the problems of the cosmos, they illuminate statements in Paul like "anyone in Christ

---

13. The problem humanity faces includes enslavement to evil powers who oppose Christ and God the Father (= four actors); the traditional reading merely posits a problem between humanity and God the Father mediated by Christ (= three actors): see Martyn, *Galatians*, 97–105 (Comment #3), 272–73 (#28), and 370–73 (#39).

14. All translations are my own unless otherwise noted. If consulted, the translation used is the NIV because my Doctorvater, Richard Longenecker, was one of its main translators.

is a new creation" (2 Cor. 5:17). There are several new Christian twists on the basic Jewish story of resurrection and the new age, so to speak.[15] But the Apocalypses do help us to understand this fundamentally Jewish way of thinking about salvation, as the scholars would say, eschatologically.[16]

3. It is now clearer than ever why we have to tell our story backward or retrospectively, in the light of Jesus's solution. Apart from his transforming work, our fleshly minds are deceived and corrupted. They are shot through with evil (Rom. 3:10–18). Anything we say about God's purposes arising out of our own location is likely to be not only baseless but also self-serving and wicked. Paul's pre-Christian life, during which he attacked the early church, is an excellent example of just this dynamic playing out (Gal. 1:13). Foundationalism is not merely ignorant. It is a plaything of the powers and so actively deceptive and manipulative.

4. We are obviously not *completely* changed by the events enacted in baptism. We are not yet perfect. The flesh persists until our deaths, and some sort of further dramatic consummation still lies ahead of us (Rom. 8:18–25). Consequently, most scholars speak of our transformation in the resurrected Christ being inaugurated.[17] But Paul is certainly confident that we possess at least a new mind (Rom. 12:2; 1 Cor. 2:16). Our "inner person" is no longer subject to the manipulations of evil powers (2 Cor. 4:16–18). Consequently, Christians have been liberated to act freely and ethically right here and right now. As we wait for our final liberation from all the burdens of the flesh, we live double lives, as creatures of two worlds, being tempted constantly to step back into the mind of the flesh, but anchored over against this in the life of the Spirit (Gal. 5:16–18, 25). "We walk by what we know to be true [and "by what we hope for"], not by what we see" (2 Cor. 5:7; see also Rom. 8:24–25).

With these further apocalyptic insights in place, we are now able to make an important connection.

---

15. (1) This resurrection takes place through Jesus; (2) it takes place, at least in some sense, now; and (3) it is open to the despised pagans.

16. See Martinus C. de Boer, *The Defeat of Death: Apocalyptic Eschatology in 1 Corinthians 15 and Romans 5*, JSNTSup 22 (Sheffield: JSOT Press, 1988); and "Paul and Jewish Apocalyptic Eschatology," in *Apocalyptic and the New Testament*, ed. Joel Marcus and Marion Soards, JSNTSup 24 (Sheffield: Sheffield Academic, 1989), 169–90.

17. This should not be understood as operating vis-à-vis the flesh in a zero-sum way. Musical analogies here will prove helpful. See my *Pauline Dogmatics*, chaps. 7 and 8, and Jeremy Begbie, "Room of One's Own? Music, Space, and Freedom," in *Music, Modernity and God: Essays in Listening* (Oxford: Oxford University Press, 2013), 141–75.

Participation

The apocalyptic starting point for Paul's analysis has revealed that we participate in Jesus's death and resurrection. These critical events underlie the salvation that drags God's great cosmic plan for communion back on track (Rom. 8:28–29). So the important scholarly emphasis on participation in Paul turns out to describe the pivotal set of events lying at the center of Paul's longer apocalyptic story. These two scholarly programs fit together like a hand in a proverbial glove (and the participatory hand should stay in the apocalyptic glove).

Scholars working on participation can now deepen our understanding of the transformational events that lie at the center of the apocalyptic gospel (compensating for what is arguably a lacuna in Martyn's work).[18] As noted, we have been changed by our participation in the death and resurrection of Jesus, possessing now, at the least, resurrected minds that know God's will and happily obey it. It follows from this that we now participate in a new, resurrected reality that shapes our ongoing behavior determinatively. So what is this exactly? Putting the same question from a slightly different angle, we must now ask what a resurrected and participatory Christian ethic looks like.

As Paul states with great insight in Romans 8:29, we are now actually beginning to participate in God's long-planned consummation of the universe in a fellowship of many siblings who bear the image of the resurrected Jesus: "God appointed us beforehand to be conformed to the image of his son, so that he might be the firstborn among many siblings." So we are participating in the divine communion (astonishing but true), and this has momentous consequences for how we are to act where we are located now, as we wait to be released from our burden of fleshly existence.[19]

This resurrected state is, in essence, a *relational* reality. It is overwhelmingly interpersonal, and, as the Trinity shows us, the key dimension to persons is their relationships.[20] Moreover, these relationships are of a par-

18. The work of Michael J. Gorman is an excellent place to begin familiarization with participatory concerns; see his *Inhabiting the Cruciform God: Kenosis, Justification, and Theosis in Paul's Narrative Soteriology* (Grand Rapids: Eerdmans, 2009), and *Becoming the Gospel: Paul, Participation, and Mission* (Grand Rapids: Eerdmans, 2015).

19. Technically, then, Paul's overarching story is supralapsarian, not infralapsarian: see Edwin Chr. van Driel, *Incarnation Anyway: Arguments for Supralapsarian Christology* (Oxford: Oxford University Press, 2008).

20. See John D. Zizioulas, *Being as Communion: Studies in Personhood and the Church*

ticular type and tenor. God's relationships are characterized fundamentally by love and by all the dynamics that facilitate and express love—behavior that is faithful, generous, forgiving, hopeful, trusting, truthful, compassionate, merciful, gentle, kind, self-controlled, and joyful (to name just some of the key dynamics).[21]

We know that God relates as love because of the revelation flowing from our participation in Jesus's death and resurrection. God loved us enough "to journey into the far country" and to assume our corrupt humanity.[22] God the Father then offered up his beloved Son to die for us, as did the Spirit, and God the Son accepted this calling obediently, suffering and dying on the cross for us, to be raised beyond this horror so that we might share in his risen life (Phil. 2:5–11). Moreover, these supremely costly actions were undertaken *while we were still sinful and hostile* (Rom. 5:5–6, 8, 10). God undertook this act of solidarity and endured its awful consequences for a corrupt humanity that rejected and repudiated it while it was happening. He died for his enemies.

This is love. Furthermore, it is covenantal in the sense that it is implacable in its determination to recall and to restore those it loves if they have fallen. It is *unconditional*. It never breaks its commitment, or abandons its relationship (Rom. 11:29). It is a love that vastly exceeds our capacity to comprehend it, hence Paul prays for spiritual enlightenment so that we might begin to grasp its true breadth, length, height, and depth (Eph. 3:14–19).[23] This is the reality that we now indwell and are called to live out of.

It is therefore critical to hold participation and apocalyptic tightly together as emphases within the same story. The revelatory starting point for our knowledge about God in Jesus, affirmed by the apocalyptic advocate, reveals that we participate in Jesus's death and resurrection. This participation reveals in turn that God loves us unconditionally and without limit

---

(Crestwood, NY: St. Vladimir's Seminary Press, 1985), 27–65 ("Personhood and Being"); and Susan G. Eastman, *Paul and the Person: Reframing Paul's Anthropology* (Grand Rapids: Eerdmans, 2017).

21. See 1 Cor. 13; Gal. 5:6, 14, 22; also Alan J. Torrance, "Is Love the Essence of God?," in *Nothing Greater, Nothing Better: Theological Essays on the Love of God*, ed. Kevin J. Vanhoozer (Grand Rapids: Eerdmans, 2001), 114–37; and my *Pauline Dogmatics*, chaps. 4 and 11.

22. Alluding here to Barth's famous and deeply moving use of Luke 15:11–32 to expound the work of Jesus on behalf of our broken humanity, in *Church Dogmatics* IV/2, § 64, 20–154.

23. See my *Framing Paul: An Epistolary Biography* (Grand Rapids: Eerdmans, 2014), 309–38, for a defense of the authenticity of "Ephesians."

as we participate in God's horrifically costly actions on our behalf while we were yet sinners. We learn that God is love "all the way down." We then need to place these insights at the heart of everything else we say about God. These truths must drive our entire story about God, humanity, and the cosmos; and where other "truths" occlude or contradict these central insights, they must be judged and either modified or rejected, even when they include things said elsewhere by Paul himself![24]

With these participatory insights now set firmly within their broader apocalyptic story, we can address a second complaint that is often directed at the apocalyptic reading.[25]

Agency

We have just learned in the strongest possible terms that God is love all the way down. And love is unconditional. The relationships it sets up are unbreakable. They do not depend on the recipients of love fulfilling conditions in the manner of a contract or an agreement. I am the parent of two children, a son and a daughter. My relationship to them, as a father, is unconditional. It will never alter. Nothing my children do can earn it, establish it, or undermine it. I will always be their father. And it is the same with God, only more so.[26]

God loves us unconditionally and so exists in an ultimately unbreakable covenant with us—a wonderful thing to celebrate. But the unconditionality of this relationship does not mean that our own freedom is being overruled, this being a concern that some critics of the apocalyptic reading have. Far from it.

24. Put slightly differently, we must think through all our other questions and challenges in the light of these basal insights, which raises the possibility of *Sachkritik* ("Sense-" or "Subject-interpretation"). All the things Paul himself said must be arraigned before the bar of the christological account of God that he himself affirmed as central. We must, if necessary, reform Pauline material in the light of Paul's gospel. This realization creates important interpretive options vis-à-vis Paul's instructions that presuppose slavery and traditional accounts of marriage and gender.

25. The first was that it ought to be oriented primarily by Jewish Apocalypses. But this program misunderstands the correct starting point for an apocalyptic reading of Paul's theology—that is, revelation—and subverts that starting point, being a type of historicizing foundationalism.

26. Insights expounded matchlessly by James B. Torrance in "Covenant or Contract: A Study of the Theological Background of Worship in Seventeenth-Century Scotland," *Scottish Journal of Theology* 23 (1970): 51–76.

The underlying problem here seems to be the anxiety raised by the use of the word *unconditional*, which conjures the specter of an unconditional account of *causality*. If God is in relationship with us, is God not acting on us? And if God acts on us, and consequently causes us to do certain things, does this not, to this degree, exclude my activity? And does it not follow that if God relates to us unconditionally, as apocalyptic readers aver, then has not *all* my activity been excluded? Have I not just been reduced, in ethical terms, to an inanimate, inert object like a rock?

Clearly, such a position would be absurd. We would not know what to do with all Paul's ethical material, and we would not even know how to act. But this is an unnecessary anxiety.

If we conceive of causality as a fixed, automatic, and even mechanical process, then this chain of reasoning would be true. Mechanical (and any related) causes do exist in a zero-sum relation with any free activity by the objects of their actions. Heat bakes clay hard. The clay has no agency. It does not choose to cooperate with the baking temperature acting on it. But there is no need to analogize God's causal influence on us in this way. We are projecting our own images onto God at this moment and so indulging again in idolatrous foundationalism. (We are projecting notions of causality from our surrounding locations, usually thinking of those locations in accordance with the insightful but deeply limited suggestions of Isaac Newton or mechanistic thinkers like him.) The correct, apocalyptic approach to this question is to let our understanding of God's causal activity on us be explained by the definitive truth about God that is Jesus. And we learn from Jesus that God's influence on people is unconditional, in the sense that God never withdraws from the relationship, and it is clearly also very powerful. But it is hardly automatic or mechanical. Jesus was not a rock, and as our Lord, he does not treat us like rocks either. Think simply of how he treated his disciples. Divine influence, whether between Father and Spirit and Son, or from God to us as seen most clearly from the Son, is *personal* and *relational*. And relationships *are influential*. They affect us, often deeply. The most important causal influence on my life is undoubtedly my spouse's relationship with me. This influences me and changes me more than anything else in my world. But numerous other people have affected me profoundly as well—my parents, teachers, friends, students, and even my enemies. Personal relationships are profoundly influential. They make us what we are. But they are the antithesis of constriction. Relationships set us free.

In new relationships we learn to do things we could not do before. Gifted performers, like Pavarotti, one of the greatest operatic tenors of all time, are only able to do what they do because they have gifted teachers who have taught them over time, nurtured them, and, in short, related to them faithfully and wisely. We see here, then, that relationships help us to grow, teaching us to do things we could not do before, thereby making us "free" to do them.

Hence it is precisely God's unconditional relationship with us in Jesus that liberates us and then gifts us with the possibility of further freedoms as we grow in righteousness and in love, by being conformed to him as he relates to us, and teaches and shapes us, over time. As Paul put it (paraphrasing a little), we can only work out our salvation with fear and trembling *because* God is working on us and in us, as well as, hopefully, through us (see Phil. 2:12–13; 1 Thess. 2:13). Ironically, then, far from struggling to account for our human agency, the apocalyptic reading of Paul, with its all-important affirmation of the unconditionality of God's relationship with us, provides the only theologically plausible account *of* our agency.[27]

With this clarification, we can turn to the third and final principal criticism made of the apocalyptic reading, finding that, once again, it points unwittingly to one of the reading's greatest strengths.

God's People

Martyn famously said that there are no through trains from the Old Testament dispensation and the church's Jewish past to the new age that begins with the disclosure of Jesus.[28] By saying so, he was trying to protect the apocalyptic account of Paul's gospel from what I call "sacred nation theology," which scholars tend to discuss under the rubric of salvation history. To grasp what is going on here, we need to appreciate that towering antecedents to the apocalyptic reading like Ernst Käsemann were shaped formatively by the same events that we noted at the outset of this essay shaped Karl Barth—National Socialism's rise to power in Germany in the

27. Again, Eastman's *Paul and the Person* should be consulted. She uses "the second personal" to illuminate the interactions here in detail. A key insight is the constitution of the person *by* relationships from infancy, first through the primary caregiver. Relationships supply people with agency. See also Andrew Pinsent, "The Non-Aristotelian Virtue of Truth from the Second-Person Perspective," *European Journal for Philosophy of Religion* 5 (2013): 87–104; and Eleanore Stump, "Omnipresence, Indwelling, and the Second-Personal," *European Journal for Philosophy of Religion* 5 (2013): 29–54.

28. Martyn, *Theological Issues*, 224.

1930s, along with its horrific aftermath. The National Socialists used a stirring nationalist narrative. They told a story about Germany as the guardian of a sacred Aryan nation that was entitled to territory, power, and status, thereby justifying a ghastly program of ethnic purification and territorial expansion—a story that was very similar to, and in part depended on, a biblical story of the sacred nation of Israel rising to territory, power, and status. This story resonated with the German people in the thirties, *and it still resonates with people today!*[29] Having experienced the catastrophe of World War II, Käsemann, Martyn, and others understandably sought to foreclose on any Pauline justification for a sacred nation narrative, and it is clearly vital to maintain this resistance vigilantly today.[30]

But we cannot simply abandon all talk of salvation history for this defense. Some story must still be told about the sacred nation that preceded Jesus. If we do not do this, we risk saying that God was not involved in creation, or in history, or in the Jews—the heresy of Marcion. In a less extreme version of this error, we make God distant and unengaged—a form of deism, behind which atheism always lurks; or we risk a form of Manichaeistic dualism, with evil in control of God's created world and his people, and God apparently not powerful enough to combat it for much of human history. So we need to tell a story about Israel, and then about Jews and Judaism, as they led up to the arrival of Jesus, as well as, ultimately, tell the story of creation that preceded this human history. But how do we tell this story so that we avoid activating sacred nation theology, which of course we must strive to reject at all costs?

The apocalyptic reading is perfectly poised to answer this challenge (and *only* the apocalyptic reading can answer it!). Sacred nation theology is simply a peculiarly vicious form of theological foundationalism. It works forward: its story of an oppressed people fighting for liberation and then for a country, derived from a reading of the Old Testament, precedes and thereby controls the coming of Jesus so that he fits into that program and legitimizes it, instead of disrupting it. We can eliminate this agenda (and eliminate its innate supersessionism) if we tell the salvation-historical story in the same way that we told the story of our human plight, *backward*. We look back from *the* Jew, Jesus, and grasp the prior history of Jews and Judaism in his

29. The same basic story justified the horrors of apartheid in South Africa from the 1950s and the ethnic cleansing carried out by Serbs in former Yugoslavia in the 1990s.

30. Käsemann had a sharp exchange with Cullmann and Stendahl. See his "Justification and Salvation History in the Epistle to the Romans," in *Perspectives on Paul*, trans. Margaret Kohl (London: SCM, 1971), 60–78.

light, retrospectively (and do the same later on with created categories; see Rom. 9:4–5, 33; 10:4; Col. 1:15–20). Jesus thereby controls our understanding of Israel and of the Jews, entailing a committed but reconciling, peaceful, and gracious account of God's people as we read them in the light of their climactic moment, Jesus (Eph. 2:14–22).[31] Israel, properly understood, is called to give life to the nations by way of its Messiah, and to point forward to the resurrection from the dead (Rom. 9:15; Gal. 3:7–9). The terrors of sacred nation theology are stripped away when Israel is viewed through the prism of Jesus's cross and resurrection—something we see Paul doing at various points in Romans (and in his other letters), as any good apocalyptic interpreter should.

And in fact it is now time to talk in more detail about Romans.

The Apocalyptic Road through Romans

How do we preach through Romans so that we interpret it apocalyptically and don't slip into dangerous foundationalisms of one sort or another?

I recommend expounding Romans in its dogmatic or theological order, beginning with the revelation of God's true nature and purposes through Jesus, rather than in its rhetorical order. Romans is not a treatise in systematic theology. It is a pastoral letter written to address pressing challenges that the Roman Christians were shortly to face. And Paul does not address these questions in Romans like a systematic theologian, with first principles discussed first. Writing to many Christians who did not actually know him, Paul addressed these challenges in their most persuasive order, so his first principles appear later in the letter, after the ground has been suitably prepared in personal terms. In order to read Romans correctly in theological terms, then, we will need to read it out of its actual order, following an alternative, apocalyptic road.

The apocalyptic road through Romans travels through several stages. To give a quick overview: it begins in chapters 5–8. Then it jumps to chapters 12–15 for a discussion about the church. It loops back to Paul's account of Judaism, in which he heavily accents Abraham and the other patriarchs and matriarchs, in chapter 4 and chapters 9–11. Then it investigates the circumstances eliciting the letter found in the letter's practical framing sections

---

31. I provide a sketch of these dynamics in my *Quest for Paul's Gospel: A Suggested Strategy* (London: T&T Clark International, 2005), 132–45 (chap. 7).

(1:1–15; 15:14–16:27), using this information to deal finally with the great problem passage for apocalyptic readings, which is chapters 1–3 (specifically 1:18–3:20). We should now take a closer look at each of these stages.

Stage 1: Beginning in Romans 5–8: The Revelation of God's Love

The great Scandinavian scholar Nils Dahl noted some time ago that 5:1–11 anticipates the arguments of 8:14–39.[32] Moreover, both sections speak unequivocally of God's love, proved in the cross. We need not fear any future, whether here on earth or cosmically, in view of the unshakable truth that God is on our side and will stop at nothing to love us and to gather us in. In the light of this revelation, we can see these truths anticipated earlier in the letter, especially in 3:23–26, which announces this argumentative agenda. We also know what to do with the revelation spoken of strategically in 1:16–17 and 3:21–22.[33] God the Father is delivering us from the prison of the flesh through the costly death of his Son, who faithfully endured the horrors of the cross so that we might be resurrected. These are statements of God's Christocentric revelation, in which the divine love is central and paramount.

Stage 2: Continuing in Romans 5–8: Christian Life in Christ

The next question that arises concerns our ongoing Christian life, which is ethical but not necessarily governed by the torah. Paul describes carefully in 5:12–8:14 how Jesus has lifted us into a new, resurrected reality, which stands in counterpoint to any life lived in the flesh, where the powers have infiltrated our condition and both seduce and enslave us—the story of Adam. Even a good thing like the torah can be manipulated by our lusts, abetted by the powers, such is the corruption of our Adamic condition. Note, however, that this does not foreclose on *God* taking up the instructions of the torah in the new, resurrected situation. So Paul can still quote the Jewish Scriptures frequently, as he does upward of

---

32. *Studies in Paul: Theology of the Early Christian Mission* (Minneapolis: Augsburg, 1977), 88–90 (Appendix I: A Synopsis of Romans 5:1–11 and 8:1–39).

33. More detail esp. concerning 1:16–17 and 3:21–26 is provided in my *The Deliverance of God: An Apocalyptic Rereading of Justification in Paul* (Grand Rapids: Eerdmans, 2009).

fifty times in Romans, but this usage must be at the behest of the Spirit. The new, resurrected mind, formed and guided by the Spirit, lives in a transcendent, relational world. So torah observance is not mandatory. Loving relationality is, however. These truths are enacted in baptism. Christians are now free to act rightly and live in two worlds. But they are summoned to reject the mentality of the flesh and to act in terms of the Spirit.

Stage 3: Continuing with Romans 12–15 and the (Diverse) Church

What comes next? The best place to go in Romans is to the more detailed description of the relational shape of the new community, which unfolds in 12:1–15:13. Paul uses the metaphor of a body to describe the nature of the community. Its leaders are gifted with various skills and roles by the Spirit and called to a particular openhanded, merciful, and considerate relationality, even to outsiders and enemies. It also emphasizes appropriately virtuous and skillful leadership. Moreover, it is *diverse*. A loving relationality can indwell different forms of life, whether more or less Jewish (so chap. 14). Some want to observe the seventh day and to follow the dietary prescriptions in the books of Moses; some do not feel so led. There is room within the community for both. *How* they relate together is more important than *what* they do.[34]

Stage 4: God's People, the Jews

Paul is under pressure to show that a community of converted pagans and messianic Jews worshiping in the same body is in fact a legitimate development of the history of God's people, the Jews (9:30–31). So he argues in two sections that when we look back on the Jews from the vantage point of God revealed as *the* Jew, Jesus, we see a history of divine words and acts of resurrection written into Israel from its inception (chap. 4; 9:6–29). From the beginning God has called his people into being, just as Isaac was born from loins and a womb that were sterile and hence biologically dead (4:17–22). The Jews, then, are at bottom the people given life by God,

---

34. A great deal more information about the community can be found in my *Pauline Dogmatics*, esp. in part 2, chaps. 9–16.

something fulfilled in Jesus's resurrection.[35] Moreover, just as the Hebrews benefited from Pharaoh's hardness of heart, and grace overflowed to them in the exodus, so too, if Jews prove hard of heart in Paul's day, grace can overflow again in an unexpected direction, this time to the pagan nations, gathering them in, and a few scriptural texts even predict this event. God is acting consistently here (9:14–26).

Stage 5: Religion and Unbelievers

Since many Jews in Paul's day continued to reject Jesus and his followers, however, we need to ask what comes next. Paul depicts a contest playing out between human resistance and God's purposes. The Jews are certainly called to respond to Jesus, like everyone else, affirming who he is, namely, the Lord. We learn from this that we are responsible for our sins, even if we are being manipulated on some level by evil powers (9:30–10:17). Paul, however, is confident that God will woo his people back, even as the majority currently resist him. In particular, the preservation of a small remnant of believing Jews shows that a full flowering forth will eventually take place, ultimately because God will never let go of his commitments and his promises to the original fathers and mothers of Israel (9:27–29; chap. 11). We learn from this that we have every reason for optimism about the future even when we are surrounded by the most incomprehensible sin—as incomprehensible as the Jews rejecting their God as he comes to them in person as their savior and messiah. In the contest between human stupidity and divine benevolence, without in any way overriding our agency—even if, as here, it is tragically misdirected—God will win! His purposes are paramount, his commitment is irrevocable, and his power is ultimately unstoppable.

Stage 6: Why Paul Wrote Romans

It is now worth putting a practical scenario in place. Although the reasons why Paul wrote Romans are much debated, only one theory can account for the letter's long engagements with various Jewish questions,

---

35. A slightly longer sketch of this narrative is provided in *Paul: An Apostle's Journey* (Grand Rapids: Eerdmans, 2018), 151–70.

when it was written by the apostle appointed by God to go to the pagans, who is writing to a primarily pagan audience. As 16:17–20 suggests directly, and 1:15 more subtly, *false teachers are heading to Rome*. We have already met these misdirected messianic Jews who attack Paul and his gospel in Galatians and in Philippians 3. At this point in the unfolding controversy, Paul is supposed to be traveling from Corinth eastward to Jerusalem to deliver a large sum of money to the church (15:23–33). He consequently expects to lose the race with his rivals westward to Rome, and so a letter has to take his place. In it, he must affirm his gospel, defend it from his enemies' criticisms, and try to take down their gospel, and we will need to sort out which discussion is which in Romans.[36]

Stage 7: False Teachers and Their False Gospel: Handling Romans 1–3

If we read Romans 1–3 in its usual way, as a self-evident demonstration of the human problem, then we introduce foundationalism into Paul's thinking from the outset, and we undermine everything that we have said up to this moment. Brunner would be right! Paul would commit, at least in Romans 1:19–20, to a fundamental role for natural theology. Moreover, since Barth is right about almost everything Paul says everywhere else, we make the apostle into a very muddled figure. Paul contradicts himself at a fundamental level. (He also gives a very unfair account of Judaism.)[37] So we need to ask if there is another, more apocalyptic, way to read Romans 1–3 in the broader context of the apocalyptic road through Romans that we have already sketched out. And I would suggest, crucially, that in fact he is taking down his enemies' gospel in 1:18–3:20, not establishing his own, and in a way well known to ancient people but less familiar to modern readers. Here he argues *Socratically*.[38]

---

36. More detail is provided in *Deliverance of God*, 469–518 (chap. 13); see also my *Framing Paul*, 37–189 (chaps. 2 and 3).

37. The concern of E. P. Sanders, which we can now resolve in a way that is far more satisfactory than the solution offered by the new perspective: see his *Paul and Palestinian Judaism* (Philadelphia: Fortress, 1977).

38. This is the thesis of *Deliverance of God*, summarized and debated in Chris Tilling, ed., *Beyond Old and New Perspectives on Paul: Reflections on the Work of Douglas Campbell* (Eugene, OR: Cascade Books, 2014), and anticipated in my *Quest for Paul's Gospel*, 233–61 (chap. 11).

Socratic attacks show how a position collapses on itself, and so they are particularly embarrassing.[39] If Paul can show in his opening discussion how the gospel of his enemies is pointless, falling in on itself, he will have scored a key victory. Read in this fashion, the entire letter integrates smoothly together as an apocalyptic reading of Paul's gospel as a whole.[40] And the overall result is a Paul who speaks with a clear voice—as the faithful and deeply insightful apostle of the apocalypse of Jesus Christ.

39. They are also the right offensive mode for apocalyptic thinkers, as attested most clearly in the Christian tradition by the work of Kierkegaard.

40. This construal detects the pompous voice of Paul's enemies in 13:1–7 as well, allowing a pro-Rome reading at face value, and a reading "from below" that subverts the original reading. See James C. Scott, *Domination and the Arts of Resistance: Hidden Transcripts* (New Haven: Yale University Press, 1990). A useful beginning for reading Rom. 13 this way is T. L. Carter, "The Irony of Romans 13," *Novum Testamentum* 46, no. 3 (2004): 209–28.

4

Romans and the Participationist Perspective

Michael J. Gorman

Does Romans still preach? Or is it a fossil, of little relevance to contemporary concerns? One way to approach this question is via an expression that peppers both Romans and other Pauline letters.

Some of Paul's most significant sentences include the brief but critical phrase "in Christ," or "in Christ Jesus":[1]

So you also must consider yourselves dead to sin and alive to God *in Christ Jesus.* (Rom. 6:11)

There is therefore now no condemnation for those who are *in Christ Jesus.* (Rom. 8:1)

So if anyone is *in Christ,* there is a new creation. (2 Cor. 5:17)

There is no longer Jew or Greek, there is no longer slave or free, there is no longer male and female; for all of you are one *in Christ Jesus.* (Gal. 3:28)

Whatever else this phrase means, it says that Christian believers and communities are located within the sphere of Christ's personal presence and power. To be in Christ is to *participate* in the life of the crucified but resurrected Lord.[2] This life of participation in Christ can also be

1. Sometimes "in the Lord" or simply "in him." Scripture quotations, unless otherwise indicated, are from the NRSV. (I have occasionally made minor changes to the NRSV, such as capitalizing "sin" and "death.")

2. For in-depth studies, see Michael J. Thate, Kevin J. Vanhoozer, and Constantine R. Campbell, *"In Christ" in Paul: Explorations in Paul's Theology of Union and Participation* (Grand Rapids: Eerdmans, 2018; orig. Tübingen: Mohr Siebeck, 2014); Athanasios Despotis, ed., *Participation, Justification, and Conversion: Eastern Orthodox Interpretation*

expressed in another succinct phrase expressing intimate association, "with him":

> Anyone united to the Lord becomes one spirit *with him*. (1 Cor. 6:17)

> If [we are God's] children, then [we are also] heirs, heirs of God and joint heirs with Christ—if, in fact, we suffer *with him* so that we may also be glorified *with him*. (Rom. 8:17)[3]

As a description of Christian existence, the phrase "in Christ" presumes an initiation: movement from *outside* Christ to *inside* Christ. E. P. Sanders called it "transfer" language.[4] This transfer/initiation itself occurs by means of participation—it is a "with Christ" experience that moves one from outside to inside Christ. In discussing justification "in Christ" (Gal. 2:17), Paul avers that "through the law I died to the law, so that I might live to God. I have been crucified *with Christ*" (Gal. 2:19). And in discussing baptism, he asks rhetorically, "Do you not know that all of us who have been baptized *into Christ Jesus* were baptized *into his death*? . . . We know that our old self was crucified *with him*" (Rom 6:3, 6).

Such phrases—into, in, and with Christ—express a fundamental aspect of Pauline theology and spirituality that is recognized by all interpreters of the apostle. For some, however, including myself, the texts containing such phrases are understood to be at the very core of Paul's life and thought. The "participationist perspective" advocated in this chapter takes its place alongside the Reformational, new, and apocalyptic perspectives. The participationist perspective should not, however, be seen as *competing with* these other views, but rather as *complementing* them. This chapter draws attention to key aspects of Paul—specifically of Romans—that are sometimes overlooked or underestimated. The participationist perspective sees

---

of Paul and the Debate between "Old and New Perspectives on Paul" (Tübingen: Mohr Siebeck, 2017); Constantine R. Campbell, *Paul and Union with Christ: An Exegetical and Theological Study* (Grand Rapids: Zondervan, 2012); and Michael J. Gorman, *Participating in Christ: Explorations in Paul's Theology and Spirituality* (Grand Rapids: Baker Academic, 2019). For pastoral implications, see J. Todd Billings, *Union with Christ: Reframing Theology and Ministry for the Church* (Grand Rapids: Baker Academic, 2011).

3. There are various ways in Greek to express "with Christ": preposition, prefix, case usage. See Campbell, *Paul and Union with Christ*.

4. E. P. Sanders, *Paul and Palestinian Judaism: A Comparison of Patterns of Religion* (Philadelphia: Fortress, 1977), esp. 463–72.

transformative participation in the resurrected crucified Messiah as transformative participation in the very life of God—Father, Son, and Spirit—and as the center of Paul's theology and spirituality.

The Participationist Pedigree

Participation is a slippery word. Later we will unpack it generally with respect to Paul and specifically regarding Romans. But first we note that this perspective has an important pedigree, with significant advocates both ancient and modern.

For many Christians, Paul's theology, especially in Romans, can be summarized as "justification by faith" or "righteousness by faith." This focus, which sees justification in terms of a courtroom verdict (juridical or juristic language), stems from readings of Paul during the Protestant Reformation—or at least from certain interpretations of those sixteenth-century readings. A focus on transformative participation, however, can already be found in the early centuries of the church, especially in the East. The influential theologians Irenaeus and Athanasius, basing their view in part on Paul, understood salvation as follows: He (God or Christ) became what we are, so that we might become what he is.[5] Even Augustine in the West held a similar view.[6]

In the Christian tradition, this understanding of salvation has often been called "deification," or "theosis": becoming like God. (It has also been called Christification, or Christosis.)[7] The basic idea of theosis or Christosis is that, by virtue of the incarnation and the work of the Spirit, we can become like Christ, which means like God, for Christ is the image of God. In other words, we become like God by participating in the life of God. Although some people object to the language of theosis or even Christosis, preferring simply "union with Christ," the understanding of salvation is similar: participation leading to transformation, both ethical and eschatological.

Many of the Protestant reformers were actually favorably disposed toward this interpretation of salvation and of Paul. For a variety of reasons,

5. See, e.g., Irenaeus, *Against Heresies* 5, Preface 1; Athanasius, *Incarnation of the Word* 54.

6. See David Vincent Meconi, *The One Christ: St. Augustine's Theology of Deification* (Washington, DC: Catholic University of America Press, 2013).

7. See Ben C. Blackwell, *Christosis: Engaging Paul's Soteriology with His Patristic Interpreters* (Grand Rapids: Eerdmans, 2016).

the Reformation emphasis on participation and transformation has often been neglected. Recently, however, there has been a great revival in the understanding of participation (union with Christ and transformation) in theologians such as John Calvin and Martin Luther.[8] These reformers did not see transformation into Christlikeness by participation in him as in any sense a denial of justification by grace through faith. In fact, it has been convincingly argued that both Calvin and Luther understood justification as dependent on union with Christ.

Early in the twentieth century, the missionary-physician and biblical scholar Albert Schweitzer famously claimed, "The doctrine of righteousness by faith [in Paul, especially Romans] is therefore a subsidiary crater, which has formed within the rim of the main crater—the mystical doctrine of redemption through being-in-Christ."[9] A half century later, E. P. Sanders began a revolution in the study of Paul by similarly claiming that Paul "is not primarily concerned with the juristic categories [of righteousness by faith]," for "the real bite of his theology lies in the participatory categories."[10] As we will see below, this appropriate emphasis on participation should not become a way of separating it from justification (as Schweitzer did) and thereby marginalizing justification; even Sanders saw a connection between the two.[11] Emphasizing participation should, however, result in a revised understanding of justification to include participation and transformation.[12]

Sanders did not fully spell out what participation entails. Subsequently, Richard Hays proposed four main elements: belonging to a family; political or military solidarity with Christ (as in Rom. 6, where Paul speaks of "weapons of righteousness"); participating in the *ekklēsia* (the "church"); and living within the Christ story ("narrative participation").[13] Elsewhere I have suggested several additional features of Paul's understanding of par-

8. See, e.g., Stephen J. Chester, *Reading Paul with the Reformers: Reconciling Old and New Perspectives* (Grand Rapids: Eerdmans, 2017).

9. Albert Schweitzer, *The Mysticism of Paul the Apostle*, trans. W. Montgomery (Baltimore: Johns Hopkins University Press, 1998 [orig. 1930]), 225.

10. Sanders, *Paul and Palestinian Judaism*, 502. He called this "participationist eschatology" (549).

11. E.g., Sanders, *Paul and Palestinian Judaism*, 440.

12. See below and my *Inhabiting the Cruciform God: Kenosis, Justification, and Theosis in Paul's Narrative Soteriology* (Grand Rapids: Eerdmans, 2009), esp. 40–104.

13. "What Is 'Real Participation in Christ'? A Dialogue with E. P. Sanders on Pauline Soteriology," in *Redefining First-Century Jewish and Christian Identities: Essays in Honor of Ed Parish Sanders*, ed. Fabian E. Udoh et al. (Notre Dame, IN: University of Notre Dame Press, 2008), 336–51.

ticipation, which marks believers from the beginning of their journey to its conclusion:[14]

- Justification by faith and baptism into Christ as participatory events of entering into life *in* Christ and *with* others (incorporation into Christ's body)
- Christian existence as intimate and exclusive communion with Christ, in which believers live in Christ/the Spirit and Christ/the Spirit lives in and among them ("mutual indwelling")
- Being in Christ as a constant process of transformation into his image, vividly expressed in the metaphor of putting on Christlike clothing
- Ongoing participation in Christ's cross, meaning especially self-giving, sacrificial love and suffering as the faithful embodiment of his story ("cruciformity")[15]
- Sharing in God's mission in Christ as both beneficiaries and partners: becoming a people that participates in the new creation by becoming the righteousness (or justice) of God and by presenting themselves to God to do God's will in the world.

We will see that each of these appears in Romans itself.[16]

Where does Paul get his idea of participation, specifically of the mutual indwelling of Christ/the Spirit and believers? Some scholars have proposed the Stoics, who believed that a spark of eternal divine Reason, the Logos, indwells all people and enables them to live in accord with Reason itself. Although there are some similarities between Paul and the Stoics, a more fruitful line of inquiry takes us back to Israel's prophets.

Ezekiel, Isaiah, and Joel all used the imagery of God's pouring out the Spirit on the people of God.[17] Ezekiel even promised that the Spirit would

---

14. Adapted from my *Becoming the Gospel: Paul, Participation, and Mission* (Grand Rapids: Eerdmans, 2015), 34.

15. See my *Cruciformity: Paul's Narrative Spirituality of the Cross* (Grand Rapids: Eerdmans, 2001).

16. Other contemporary Pauline scholars—Protestant, Anglican, Roman Catholic, and Eastern Orthodox—have also emphasized the centrality of participation in Paul, including (in addition to Sanders and Hays) James D. G. Dunn (new perspective); Douglas Campbell and Susan Eastman (apocalyptic perspective); and Ben Blackwell, Athanasios Despotis, Morna Hooker, Andy Johnson, Thomas Stegman, and Udo Schnelle (participationist perspective per se).

17. Isa. 32:15; Ezek. 36; 39:29; Joel 2:28.

be placed *within* the people of God, resurrecting them to new life (Ezek. 36:26–27; 37:1–14). The "liquid" metaphor of pouring and the promise of internalization are robust images of participation. Such images are adopted by John the Baptist, Jesus, and the earliest Christians (including Paul), being complemented with the "liquid" images of filling, immersion (baptism), and drinking. These images of the Spirit's liquidity dramatically portray the total absorption of believers into the Spirit's transformative activity. The result of these various complementary metaphors is an understanding of total participation in the Spirit, who resides—like the air we breathe—both inside and outside believers.

The association of this language not only with the Spirit but also with Christ himself most likely took place because the earliest Christians understood the Spirit to have been at work in Jesus's earthly ministry and to be the means of Jesus's ongoing postresurrection presence in the world. Thus Paul can say that we have been baptized "in the one Spirit . . . into one body," the body of Christ (1 Cor. 12:13; cf. Rom. 6:3; Gal. 3:27). To get intimately ("liquidly") involved with the Spirit is to get intimately involved with the Messiah, for the Spirit is both the Spirit of God (the Father) and the Spirit of Christ (the Son; Gal. 4:6; Rom. 8). Moreover, it is likely that because Jews and early Christians understood the Messiah to embody the righteousness of God, the natural implication would be that those "in" the Messiah would do so too. That this righteousness would be cruciform probably derived in part from Jesus's interpretation of his death as a baptism in which his disciples would share (Mark 10:38–39).

Romans and Participation: Getting Started

Paul's Letter to the Romans is . . . a letter. If that is stating the obvious, it still needs to be stressed. Although Romans is arguably the most influential Christian letter ever penned, it is a real letter addressed to real people facing real issues. It is not primarily a systematic treatment of justification, participation in Christ, or any other theological topic. Nevertheless, Romans does possess a systematic quality because Paul wrote the letter without having been to Rome and without knowing many of his addressees. Thus Paul explicates his gospel in detail, and this pastoral letter is therefore also a rich theological document.

Perhaps the central practical issue Paul addresses in Romans is "What does it mean to be a diverse community of gentiles and Jews who have believed this gospel of the crucified and resurrected Messiah and been baptized into him?" This deceptively simple question requires a complex response, which we will examine section by section, focusing on the motif of participation.

Romans 1–4 and Participation in Christ

THE OPENING AND THEME: 1:1–17

Scholars debate whether the "thesis" of Romans is in 1:1–5 or in 1:16–17. Actually, both summarize Paul's gospel and hence his main claim. In 1:1–5 the emphasis lies on the royalty and resurrection of Jesus, which requires a response called "the obedience of faith" (see also 16:26),[18] while in 1:16–17 the focus is on God's saving power (which rescues humanity from Sin and Death), or God's righteousness (restorative justice), expressed "through faith for faith" (1:17).

We learn in both 1:5 and 1:17 that faith will be a major concern of this letter. Both verses have elicited significant scholarly discussion. Does the phrase in 1:5 mean "the obedience that arises from faith," "faithful obedience," or something else? Does 1:17 refer to receiving God's righteousness through human faith from start to finish? Or does it possibly mean that *God's* righteousness was revealed through *Christ's* faith (i.e., his faithfulness unto death) in order to elicit *our* faith(fulness)?

If we tentatively accept the proposal that 1:17 refers to Christ's faithful death that generates our response of faithfulness, then we can also plausibly suggest that the two key words in 1:5—*obedience* and *faith*—echo Paul's interpretation of Christ's death. That death was Christ's act of obedience, in contrast to Adam's (and our) disobedience (5:12–21), and his act of faithfulness, in contrast to Israel's (and our) unfaithfulness.[19] In other words, Paul sees his mission, enabled by grace, as proclaiming Christ's obedience/faithfulness in order to elicit a similar obedience/faithfulness from his hearers.[20] We might even call this faith "believing allegiance."[21] As we will see throughout Romans, this is neither "works righteousness" nor

18. Rom. 1:5 and 16:26 constitute the letter's literary bookends.

19. We will discuss the "faithfulness of Christ" in Rom. 3:22, 26 below. Israel's unfaithfulness and God's faithfulness are detailed in Rom. 9–11.

20. See also 6:15–20; 10:16; 15:18.

21. See, e.g., Matthew W. Bates, *Salvation by Allegiance Alone: Rethinking Faith, Works, and the Gospel of Jesus the King* (Grand Rapids: Baker Academic, 2017).

merely "imitation," since it can only happen in Christ and by the working of the Spirit of holiness manifested in Jesus's resurrection (1:4). That is, Paul's mission is to effect Spirit-enabled participation in the faithful obedience of the crucified and resurrected Messiah Jesus, and thus in the righteousness of God, among the nations.

ROMANS 1:18–3:20 AND THE NEED FOR PARTICIPATION

Romans 1:18–3:20 is a stinging indictment of humanity, both gentiles and Jews. It portrays the human condition as one that we have brought on ourselves, but one from which we cannot extract ourselves. We have failed to honor God as God, and the result has been various idolatries and immoralities, as the mistreatment of God has also led to the mistreatment of others. Humanity has become covenantally dysfunctional, unwilling and unable to love God or love neighbor as God intended.

The theological and rhetorical climax of 1:18–3:20 occurs in 3:9–18, which includes these words:

> We have already charged that all, both Jews and Greeks, are under the power of Sin, as it is written:
> "There is no one who is righteous, not even one . . .
> there is no one who seeks God . . .
> there is no one who shows kindness . . ."
> ". . . and the way of peace they have not known."
> "There is no fear of God before their eyes."
> (Rom 3:9–18)

Humans are not just sinners in need of repentance and forgiveness; our sins, which stretch from head to toe (3:13–18), are symptoms of a more fundamental problem. We are slaves to Sin, which Paul portrays as both an oppressive external power, as here, and a controlling internal force, as in Romans 7: "Now if I do what I do not want, it is no longer I that do it, but Sin that dwells within me" (7:20). We are oppressed by the power of Sin in which we dwell and which dwells in us: a mutual indwelling. Those who fail to glorify God have lost the glory of God (3:23)—the holy divine splendor that was shared with Israel and thereby available to the nations—and have been invaded by another presence.

This, then, is a "no exit" situation, humanly speaking, a condition of Sin and sins rather than holiness, of Death rather than life. It can only be fixed by a divine incursion, a benign invasion of liberation. With this assessment, the participationist perspective agrees with the apocalyptic perspective. We must stress, however, that this divine incursion needs to happen, not only into the human condition, but especially into each human heart. The dual reality of externally overpowering and indwelling Sin must be replaced by a new dual reality, the externally empowering and indwelling Spirit of God/Christ. Paul alludes to this already in 2:28 when he refers to the need for everyone to receive the heart circumcision promised by God in Deuteronomy 30:6.

This promise resonates, in turn, with the prophetic new-covenant promises: God will put his law within his people, writing it on their hearts (Jer. 31:33); he will put his Spirit within them, replacing their heart of stone with a heart of flesh, and enabling them to follow his statutes (Ezek. 36:26–27).[22] Such prophetic texts make it clear that covenantal dysfunctionality can be overcome only by a radical form of participation: the gift of God's own self, by his Spirit, into human hearts—the infilling of the divine presence to enable covenant faithfulness. As we will see below, Paul says that this is precisely what God has done: after lovingly giving us his Son to embody the covenant in his faithful and loving death, he has lovingly poured out his Spirit into our hearts so that the covenant might be embodied in us (Rom. 5:5; 8:3–4).

ROMANS 3:21–4:25 AND THE REALITY OF PARTICIPATION

Whether or not justification is the "heart" of Paul's gospel and of Romans, it is clearly important to Paul, particularly in Galatians, Romans, and the Corinthian letters. Yet the actual meaning of justification for Paul is disputed. Is it primarily a divine declaration, a verdict of acquittal or forgiveness for individual sinners? Or is it also, or even primarily, a declaration about admission to the people of God without the requirement of circumcision? Or is it an apocalyptic act of divine deliverance?

The participationist approach to justification does not deny that Paul understands justification, in part, in all of these ways. But it does suggest that none describes justification fully. Our contribution is to highlight the participatory and transformative character of justification according to Paul. We see this aspect of justification in two main ways in 3:21–4:25.

First, Paul's dense exposition of God's solution to the human predicament in 3:21–26 involves participation: Jesus's faithfulness and our shar-

22. See also Deut. 10:16; Jer. 4:4; 9:23–26.

ing in that faithfulness constitute the *means* and the *mode*, respectively, of justification. This claim takes us into an intense debate about Pauline phrases like *pistis Christou*, which can be translated as either "faith in Christ" or "the faith [meaning "faithfulness"] of Christ." Richard Hays, N. T. Wright, and I, among numerous other interpreters, have argued that "the faith of Christ" is the better translation. Such a phrase appears twice in this passage. In 3:22 the righteousness (or justice) of God is described as being "through the faith of Jesus Christ" (the means) and "for all who have faith" (the mode).[23] That this response of human faith to Christ's faith is more than intellectual assent, but is participatory in nature, becomes clear in the second such phrase: in 3:26 Paul avers that God justifies "the one who shares in the faithfulness of Jesus," not merely "has faith in Jesus." The Greek phrase is parallel to the description in 4:16 of those who are justified: they "share the faith of Abraham." Faith, then, is a total identification with the death of Jesus; it is, in fact, a death experience that is expressed in baptism as co-crucifixion with Jesus (Rom. 6:3–11).

Together, these two "faith of Christ" phrases suggest that justification itself is more than a divine acquittal, for participation involves transformation. We will see this made explicit in Paul's accounts of Abraham and of baptism, where we learn that death leads to life. But even here in 3:21–26, the righteousness of God manifested in the faithfulness of Christ is clearly transformative. As we saw in 1:18–3:20, God's repairing of the human condition necessitates dealing with both sins (transgressions) and Sin (the power). Humans need forgiveness and liberation, and Jesus's death provides both, for it is both a "sacrifice of atonement" (3:25)[24] and a "redemption," or liberation from slavery (3:24). Paul will unpack the meaning of this liberation more fully in chapter 6, but even here we see that justification is certainly not a "legal fiction," or even simply a change in status; it is the beginning of participating in a new reality—a new creation (2 Cor. 5:17; Gal. 6:15).

Second, Abraham's justification by faith is a fully participatory event—a death-and-resurrection experience that is the prototype of justification by means of participating in Christ's death and resurrection (see 4:25; 6:1–11). Many people have understood Paul's exposition of Abraham's faith in chapter 4 as highlighting several key aspects of justification: it is by God's

---

23. My translation here and for 3:26 below.
24. So NRSV, NIV. "Expiation" is also possible (RSV, NAB).

grace, not human works or the law or circumcision; it is received by faith (meaning trust); it consists of having righteousness "credited"; and it results in the forgiveness of sins.

All of these are (at least partially) true. But they do not go far enough—literally. Such an interpretation of Abraham and justification focuses too heavily on the first half of Romans 4, especially on the accounting metaphor found in the language of "reckoning." To be sure, this is biblical language taken from Genesis 15 and Psalm 32. It speaks of the *necessity* and *function* of faith, with the resulting forgiveness. But Paul's story of Abraham continues in the second half of chapter 4, where we learn more about the *nature* and *content* of faith and its resulting transformation. Abraham's faith was completely self-involving—indeed, it was an experience of death and resurrection. His own body was "already as good as dead," and Sarah's womb was barren—equally dead (4:19). Yet God delivered on his promise, and Sarah delivered Isaac. For Jews in Paul's day, the continuation of the family meant no less than resurrection and eternal life. Abraham's being made "the father of many nations" is the work of the God who "gives life to the dead and calls into existence the things that do not exist" (4:17). To "share the faith of Abraham" (4:16) is to go through a similar experience of death and resurrection by identifying with God's gracious act in the death and resurrection of Jesus (4:23–26). Justification requires not only Jesus's death but also his resurrection, because it is a participation in—a baptism into (chap. 6)—both events; it is an event of resurrection emerging from death, just as it was for Abraham.

Romans 5–8 and Participation in Christ

ROMANS 5:1–11 AND PARTICIPATION DIVINE AND HUMAN

Romans 5:1–11 is a significant bridge between chapters 1–4 and the rest of chapters 5–8. Paul summarizes the past, present, and future dimensions of the new life of righteousness and reconciliation made possible by God's gracious, loving treatment of humanity gone astray. This love is known *experientially* by means of the Spirit, who has been poured into believers' hearts (5:5), fulfilling the prophets' promises. The gift of the Spirit is not something separate from justification but rather an integral part of it. This same divine love was manifested *publicly* in Christ's death on the cross—a death for enemies (5:6–10; cf. 8:39). In other words, our participation in the life of the Father, Son, and Spirit is made possible only by God's own participation in our lives; the initiative is God's.

This divine act of enemy-love Paul describes in terms of both "justification" and "reconciliation." These are not two distinct acts but one reality: as we have seen, justification is more than a court verdict, for it is ultimately a relational reality, the end of enmity and the beginning of a new life with God. The image of God's "pouring" the Spirit into our hearts—the core of our humanity and the seat of our will—reinforces this relational and transformational reality.

The telos, or future dimension, of this new life is also expressed in two terms: (the hope of) "glory" and "salvation." The glory that humanity has lost (3:23) will be fully restored (5:2), but the process of getting from here to there will involve suffering; it could not be otherwise for those who inhabit a Christ who was crucified and are indwelt by *his* Spirit (8:3–5; cf. 8:17–39). Yet all is not now doom and gloom, for there is joy even in this suffering (5:3; 14:17). Indeed, although the fullness of glory and salvation are future realities, Paul will later declare that "in hope we were saved" (8:24) and that the justified have been "glorified" (8:30). That is, there is a seamless (though bumpy!) process of "being transformed into the same image"—Christ, the image of God—from glory to glory (2 Cor 3:18).

The "bridge" that is Romans 5:1–11 leads us into three successive passages showing the contrast between life outside and life inside Christ. In 5:12–21 this contrast is depicted in terms of Adam versus Christ; in 6:1–7:6 it is portrayed in terms of slavery to Sin versus slavery to God/righteousness; and in 7:7–8:39 it is described in terms of life in Sin and the flesh versus life in Christ and the Spirit.

ROMANS 5:12–21 AND TRANSFORMATION IN CHRIST

The story of Adam versus Christ (5:12–21) is one of stark antithesis: Adam's act of sin and disobedience leading to condemnation and death, on the one hand, and Christ's act of righteousness and obedience (his death), characterized as God's grace, leading to righteousness and life, on the other. This passage is sometimes seen as proof that justification is, after all, simply about acquittal. There is certainly such language present, and acquittal (or forgiveness) is part of the effect of Christ's death, as we saw in 3:21–26. But this text is above all about transformation: about life rather than death, about righteousness rather than sin. It is about victory—a life not of defeat by the apocalyptic powers of Sin and Death, but of "reign[ing] in life"

(5:17 NIV, RSV), liberated for righteousness, through and in Christ. That, according to Paul—here, in chapter 6, and throughout Romans—is the power of the gospel.

Romans 6 and Participation in the Gospel Narrative

Romans 6 (or 6:1–7:6) is sometimes understood primarily as an exposition of baptism. Although this interpretation is partially correct, it is better to view the chapter as Paul's unpacking of the meaning of justification in terms of death and resurrection (from chap. 4), a reality appropriately expressed by the physical, drenching act of baptism. Nothing could be more participatory for a person than immersion into water; so too baptism is the fullest possible immersion into Christ, a full identification with him and his story. More concretely, the language of dying and rising with Christ in baptism is Paul's way of saying two main things: first, that initiation into Christ is a "death" to one way of existence and a "resurrection" to a new way of life; and second, that this initiation is a participation in the story of Christ.

Paul had reminded the Corinthians that the gospel he received and proclaims is summarized in a sort of mini-creed consisting of four main acts in a dramatic salvation narrative: Christ's death, burial, resurrection, and postresurrection appearances (1 Cor. 15:3–9). This drama reappears in participatory mode in Romans 6. Believers enter into the narrative and participate in each act:[25]

DRAMATIC ACT	THE STORY OF CHRIST (1 COR. 15)	THE STORY OF BELIEVERS (ROM. 6)
Death	Christ died for our sins in accordance with the scriptures (15:3)	We . . . died to Sin . . . were baptized into his death (6:2–3); we have been united with him in a death like his (6:5); our old self was crucified with him (6:6); we have died with Christ (6:8); dead to Sin (6:11)

25. Adapted from my *Apostle of the Crucified Lord: A Theological Introduction to Paul and His Letters*, 2nd ed. (Grand Rapids: Eerdmans, 2017), 433.

DRAMATIC ACT	THE STORY OF CHRIST (1 COR. 15)	THE STORY OF BELIEVERS (ROM. 6)
Burial	he was buried (15:4a)	we have been buried with him by baptism into death (6:4)
Resurrection	he was raised on the third day in accordance with the scriptures (15:4b)	*Present (resurrection to new life):* just as Christ was raised from the dead . . . so we too might walk in newness of life (6:4); alive to God in Christ Jesus (6:11; cf. 6:13)
		Future (bodily resurrection): we will certainly be united with him in a resurrection like his (6:5); we will also live with him (6:8)
Appearances	he appeared to Cephas, then to the twelve, then to others (15:5–9)	present yourselves to God as those who have been brought from death to life (6:13)[26]

In other words, believing the gospel (or affirming the creed) is not merely assenting to its truths but participating in its story or, more precisely, participating in the reality the story narrates. "Believing," then, actually means "becoming"; to believe and be baptized is to be transformed, through a death and resurrection, into something altogether new. And in so becoming, believers (the baptized) enact the story, step by step, as a "living exegesis" of it, starting at baptism and continuing throughout life.

Besides death and resurrection, the other major image in Romans 6 is that of slavery. Paul elaborates on the claims of chapter 3 that humanity is enslaved to Sin (leading to death) but liberated from Sin by God's grace in Christ (6:6–7, 11, 17–18). The verb in verse 7 (Greek *dedikaiōtai*), in fact, suggests that justification is closely linked to baptism, and that liberation from Sin is an essential aspect of justification/baptism. Paradoxically, this liberation is a new form of slavery, not to Sin but to God/righteousness

---

26. See similar language about Jesus's appearances in Acts 1:3, using the same Greek verb translated "present."

(6:13–22). To be in Christ, baptized into the Lord who made himself a slave for our sakes (Phil. 2:6–11), is to constantly present oneself and one's bodily members in service to God, who is both the liberator and the new Lord (6:13, 16, 19). The telos, or final destination, of this holy way of life in Christ is eternal life in him (6:22–23). In other words, Romans 6 tells us that, in Christ, Sin and Death are replaced by Righteousness and Life; participation in him means the restoration of God's glory: holiness (new life) and immortality (eternal life).

Romans 7–8 and Participation in the Life of Father, Son, and Spirit

As noted earlier, Paul's portrayal of the human predicament involves humanity's being covenantally dysfunctional by virtue of the external and internal presence of the apocalyptic power Sin. The death of Christ is an act of both expiation (forgiveness) and liberation, such that those restored to right covenant relationship with God may experience a resurrection-like life that comes, paradoxically, by means of remaining crucified with Christ. In chapters 7 and 8 of Romans (or, more precisely, 7:7–8:39), Paul spells out the practical differences between life in the flesh, under the power of indwelling Sin, and life in Christ, under the power of the indwelling Spirit.[27] As in Romans 6, Paul again uses the language of slavery and liberation as well as the language of intimate participation.

This portrayal of the participatory life in Christ has three principal dimensions: the mutual indwelling of believers and Christ/the Spirit; believers' adoption as God's children; and the Christ-shaped pattern of suffering followed by glorification that is central to life with the Father, Son, and Spirit.

In Christ/In the Spirit, and Christ/the Spirit Within

Romans 8 is a text bursting with life and hope after the despair articulated in chapter 7. The opening proclamation of "No condemnation!" is not simply the announcement of a divine courtroom verdict. It is emphatically connected to the reality of being "in Christ Jesus" (8:1), where "the law of the Spirit of life in Christ Jesus has set you free from the law of Sin and of

---

27. Here the "flesh" is not the body but the powerful reality that opposes God's Spirit and God's purposes for human life.

Death" (8:2). Humanity's enslavement to Sin (the power within and without [7:13–24]) and its consequence of Death, both present and eternal, have been reversed by the Father's dual sending of the Son and the Spirit (8:3–4; cf. Gal. 4:4–6). God has accomplished what we could not: the death of his Son ended the reign of Sin by means of his faithful obedience (see also 3:21–26; 5:12–21), and the gift of the Spirit, unseating the resident power of Sin, now makes possible our own faithful obedience (1:5; 16:26) as "the just requirement of the law" is "fulfilled in us, who walk not according to the flesh but according to the Spirit" (8:4).

Not surprisingly, Paul depicts this new life in Christ as an experience of resurrection, both present and future (8:10–11), as in chapter 6. This is because the Spirit is the divine breath of life, as Ezekiel 36–37 and other scriptural texts indicate. This same Spirit also enables obedience, as God had promised (Ezek. 36:27), for it is in covenant faithfulness that true life is found (e.g., Deut. 30).

This Spirit is both the Spirit of God (the Father) and the Spirit of the Son (8:9). The result is the articulation of a profound spirituality of mutual indwelling that involves both Christ and the Spirit. Believers are in Christ, and Christ is in them; they are in the Spirit, and the Spirit is in them (8:1–2, 9–10). The practical result of this dual sense of mutual indwelling is that to live "according to [Greek *kata*] the Spirit" (8:4–5, 12–13) means living "in accordance with [Greek *kata*] Christ Jesus" (15:5; more on this below).

"Adoption" as God's Children

If being in Christ/the Spirit is one aspect of participation highlighted in Romans 8, another is adoption. In the Roman context, adoption meant the full inclusion of the adopted child into the adopting family, involving benefits both present (relational intimacy) and future (an inheritance). Both are present in this passage: the Spirit-enabled intimate cry, in the language of Jesus, of "Abba! Father" and the promise of being "co-heirs" with Christ in a future glory.

Western readers of these texts may be tempted to take them in a highly individualistic manner. But Paul is using plural pronouns and verbs, not singular, because he is speaking of participation in a family. To be in Christ is to be together with siblings, in community, and to participate in the fellowship of the Spirit as the one body of Christ (1 Cor. 12; Phil. 2:1–4). Many of the church fathers connected this Pauline notion of being God's adopted children as a promise of deification, or theosis. In contemporary language, we might say that the Spirit enables family resemblance to Christ the elder brother and ultimately, therefore, to God the Father. But what does such family resemblance entail?

WITH CHRIST, THE SPIRIT, AND THE FATHER

Perhaps the most stunning expression of Paul's participatory theology and spirituality in Romans 8 is the cluster of "co-" words (Greek *syn-* and related forms) that appear in the chapter. Paul expresses the intimacy of believers' identification with Christ and the Spirit in the following words (often translated as "with" in English):

- *symmartyrei* (8:16; "co-witness" [of the Spirit])
- *synklēronomoi* (8:17; "co-heirs")
- *sympaschomen* (8:17; "co-suffer")
- *syndoxasthōmen* (8:17; "be co-glorified")
- *systenazei* and *synōdinei* (8:22; "co-groan" and "co-agonize" [of creation])
- *synantilambanetai* (8:26; "co-take hold of"; i.e., "help" [of the Spirit])
- *synergei* (8:28; "co-works" [of God])
- *symmorphous* (8:29; "co-formed"; cf. Phil. 3:10, 21).

This cluster of "co-" terms reveals that being in Christ entails intimate participation in the life of the Father, Son, and Spirit. It is God, of course, who initiates and blesses this participation: the Spirit bears witness with our spirits and comes to our aid in prayer; the Father works all things together for good, specifically the good of conforming us to the image of his Son.

We have already seen that for Paul living *in* Christ means living *according to* Christ. Specifically, this means Spirit-enabled, intimate identification with the story of Jesus that can be summarized in the term "co-formed" or "conformed" to Christ, especially to his suffering and death in the present and to his resurrection glory in the future (8:29–30). That is, as in Romans 6, believers participate in Christ by embodying his story. The essence of Pauline spirituality is a life of cruciformity—self-giving love, even to the point of suffering—followed by glorification. This is a scriptural narrative pattern of humiliation leading to exaltation (e.g., Isa. 52:13–53:12) and is robustly and definitively embodied in Jesus (Phil. 2:6–11).

Two final points about Romans 8. First, the church's life of suffering and groaning is a participation not only with the Spirit but also with all creation. Second, as in Romans 5, this present painful existence is ultimately hopeful, for the love of God displayed in Christ guarantees the liberation, redemption, and glorification, not only of reconciled humanity (8:31–39), but also of all creation (8:21).

Romans 9–11 and Participation in Christ

In Romans 9–11 Paul addresses the troubling reality that so few of his fellow Jews have believed the gospel. Does this mean that God is unfaithful? "Of course not!" Paul responds, utilizing more than thirty scriptural texts to prove his point and to claim that eventually "all Israel will be saved" (11:26)—though that phrase has generated plenty of debate. God's mercy, says the apostle, is indeed mysterious, but it is praiseworthy (11:25–36).

Participatory language per se is not prominent in these chapters, but one phrase and one key image are critical to note. First, Paul begins the discussion by claiming that he is "speaking the truth in Christ" (9:1) when he expresses his deep anguish at Israel's unbelief. It is significant that Paul quite naturally thinks of himself and all that he does as "in Christ." This is his fundamental understanding of what we today would call a "Christian," any and all who "confess with [their] lips that Jesus is Lord and believe in [their] heart that God raised him from the dead" (10:9).[28]

Second, the famous image in chapter 11 of God's people as an olive tree reminds us that being in Christ—in the Jewish Messiah—is both a corporate and a historical reality. Individuals are like branches, broken off (unbelieving Jews) or grafted in (believing gentiles and Jews) to God's people across time (11:11–24). The image of being "grafted in" obviously means participation, not in a narrow, privatistic sense, but as part of God's great mission in the world that is rooted in the story of Israel.

Romans 12–16 and Participation in the "In-Christ" Community

Most interpreters see a major shift in Romans at 12:1 from theology to praxis, though Paul certainly sees them as inseparable. Chapters 12–15 contain a rather comprehensive depiction of the life appropriate to an "in-Christ" community: the "one body in Christ" (12:4–5; cf. 1 Cor. 12) that con-

28. See also 15:17; 16:3, 7, 9–10.

sists of gentile and Jew, male and female, slave and free (Gal. 3:28). As chapter 14 makes clear, the church—or, rather, the various "house churches"—in Rome can express its God-given unity only in the real world of diversity. Even more important than this diversity-in-unity, however, is the necessity of the church(es) that are *in* Christ to live *according to* Christ (15:5).

This basic message can be found already in 12:1–2: "I appeal to you [plural] therefore, brothers and sisters, by the mercies of God, to present your bodies as a [singular] living sacrifice, holy and acceptable to God, which is your [plural] spiritual worship. You [plural] must not be conformed to this age, but must be transformed by the renewing of your minds, so that you [plural] may discern what is the will of God—what is good and acceptable and perfect" (NRSV, slightly altered). The Greek verb translated "present" has already been used five times in 6:13–19, all in the plural. The connection is important: the chapters to come will flesh out the life of individual and especially communal self-presentation to God that those baptized into Christ are called to embody. This is their "living sacrifice"; that is, their bodies—the place of divine worship—constitute not only the single body of Christ but also the temple of the Spirit (Rom. 8; 1 Cor. 3:16; 6:19), the locus of God's glory on earth.

But what specifically does such a Spirit-infused, multicultural worshiping community look like? Fundamentally, it will be Christlike, and specifically cruciform, for each individual and the church as a whole has been co-crucified with Christ and co-raised with him to new life in the Spirit, a life marked by the pattern of cross and resurrection, as we saw in chapter 8. This will be a community of obedient faithfulness issuing in generous love and expectant hope. Such a community will demonstrate a preferential option for the weak and will accept cultural differences about diet and other matters that do not ultimately matter (14:1–15:13). Why? Because "the kingdom of God is not food and drink but righteousness [or justice] and peace and joy in the Holy Spirit" (14:17).

A vivid image of this communal participation in Christ is that of "wearing" Christ: "[You all must] put on the Lord Jesus Christ, and make no provision for the flesh, to gratify its desires" (13:14). Similar to the opposition of the Spirit and the flesh in chapters 7–8, this antithesis makes it clear that being in Christ means taking on Christlike attitudes and practices (cf. Phil. 2:5). The image of putting Christ on, like clothing, suggests the inseparability of Christ and believers, as we—his body—are being transformed into his image (2 Cor. 3:18, using the same passive verb of transformation as in 12:2). The parallel language of putting on "the armor of light" in 13:12 is a reminder that life in Christ is a kind of spiritual, indeed apocalyptic, warfare. The enemy seeks to destroy both individuals and communities, and must be opposed, not with violence (see 12:14–21), but with Christlike practices.

A final word about the *missional* character of participating in Christ. In chapters 15 and 16 Paul speaks of himself and others as those who are in Christ and "work[ing] for God" (15:17). It would be wrong, however, to think that Paul is limiting the missional activity of the church to himself and his colleagues. Rather, an in-Christ community is inherently missional, participating in the divine mission of reconciling people to God and to one another. This is expressed in simple but significant ways: "Welcome one another, therefore, just as Christ has welcomed you, for the glory of God" (15:7) means practicing Christlike hospitality, and "Do not repay anyone evil for evil, but take thought for what is noble in the sight of all . . . [and] live peaceably with all" (12:17–18) means practicing Godlike enemy-love (see 5:6–11) in the world.

Conclusion and Reflections

Romans is an amazing pastoral letter and theological document that can be read with profit from a variety of perspectives. But for the pastor in the pulpit and the person in the pew, an emphasis on participation is absolutely critical to a theologically and spiritually healthy reading of the letter. I say this for two principal reasons.

First, as Susan Eastman has recently demonstrated in a highly insightful book on what it means to be human according to Paul (written in dialogue with modern science and psychology), participation, imitation, and relationality are at the core of human personhood.[29] Appreciating and appropriating Paul's emphasis on participation jibes with the soul's deepest longing: the desire to share in something that transcends ourselves and unites us both to God and to one another. Paul, of course, names that "something" as the life of the triune God manifested especially in the death and resurrection of Jesus.

Second, many people have learned to read Romans in a deficient way. For some, the letter contains "the Roman Road," a series of verses, isolated from their contexts, that (allegedly) present the main tenets of the gospel

29. Susan Grove Eastman, *Paul and the Person: Reframing Paul's Anthropology* (Grand Rapids: Eerdmans, 2017).

and thus the route to (individual) salvation, generally meaning postmortem eternal life. For others, Romans is a guide not only to individual justification but also to sanctification, yet this too is generally (mis)understood individualistically. Newer approaches to Romans can help correct these sorts of misreadings, and the participationist perspective offers a distinctive corrective.

This chapter stresses that Romans is about transformative participation in the life of the Father, Son, and Spirit. Paul articulates this in various ways throughout the letter: justification as transformation; dying and rising with Christ; the mutual indwelling of believers and Christ/the Spirit; the obedience of faith; individual and communal offering of selves and bodies to God; gentiles and Jews sharing in the shalom and joy of God's kingdom; believers also sharing in creation's pain and its hope for salvation. All of these together constitute a human being fully alive, which (said Irenaeus) is the glory of God. Christification is humanization.

For contemporary Christian communities, emphasizing transformative participation means we should never separate justification from sanctification, for God's saving purpose for humanity is to bring about a people characterized by faithful obedience. Furthermore, we must remember (and practice!) the truth that life in Christ is both an individual and a communal reality—a community of unity-in-diversity in touch with the wider creation's suffering. This life, moreover, cannot be properly lived without the indwelling of Christ by the Spirit, who makes Christian individuals and communities Christlike, meaning especially cross-shaped. Alive to and in Christ, the church becomes a living exegesis of Romans and of the gospel, a credible witness to an incredulous world.

And that preaches.

PREACHING ROMANS:
SERMONS

Reformational Perspective

5

Romans as Ecclesial Theology:
Building Multiethnic Missional Churches

Michael F. Bird

Paul's Epistle to the Romans is arguably the densest and most debated book of the New Testament. It is a delight to read, but it is hard work to teach through and preach from. Almost every paragraph contains caverns of controversy, but also theological gems for those who dare to dig deep enough into those caverns to find them. There are so many famous and favorite verses that we can recall, like "But God proves his love for us in that while we still were sinners Christ died for us" (Rom. 5:8) or "I appeal to you therefore, brothers and sisters, by the mercies of God, to present your bodies as a living sacrifice, holy and acceptable to God, which is your spiritual worship" (Rom. 12:1).[1] Studying Romans is daunting yet rewarding.

What Is Romans About?

But what is Romans really about? What is the big idea behind the letter? And what is the main thing we should take away from it?

A common view in evangelical circles is that Romans is about the road to salvation, sinners discovering the love and mercy of God, so much so that you can sweep up several verses from the letter to create a charming little evangelical tract about how to get saved. The Roman road to salvation usually goes something like this:

1. All have sinned and fall short of the glory of God (3:23).
2. The punishment for sin is eternal death (6:23).
3. The free gift of God is eternal life through Jesus (6:23 again).
4. People are saved by confessing with their lips that Jesus Christ is Lord (10:9).
5. Those who are justified through faith have peace with God (5:1).

---

1. Scripture quotations, unless otherwise indicated, are from the NRSV.

I'm partly sympathetic to this perspective. After all, Paul in this letter does say a lot about the gospel, about God, about atonement, about faith, about salvation and eternal life. But the fallacy of composition tells us to beware of the view that what is true of the part is really true of the whole. Yes, parts of Romans do tell us how to get saved, but that does not mean that this is the main point of the whole letter. Christian blogger and scholar Andrew Perriman points out the deficiencies of the Roman road of salvation. "To start with," he says, "you can hardly call it a road. Someone has dug up half-a-dozen paving stones from Paul's argument and laid them in a line. That's not a road. It's not even much of a path."[2]

I want to suggest to you that Romans has a different purpose and a different application, beyond an artificially constructed neo-Puritan and hyper-individualist account of salvation, something far more profound to my mind. I submit to you that Romans is really about creating a messianic missional community where, despite painful differences and manifold diversities, there is a reciprocal acceptance of one another and a shared commitment to unity. Paul's Letter to the Romans is really a missional letter that calls on the Jews and gentiles in the Roman churches to be united in the gospel, to receive one another in faith, and to come together to support the spread of the apostolic preaching of Jesus to the ends of the earth.

For the Jew First and Also for the Greek

This theme of unity, specifically the interlocking destinies of Jews and gentiles in Christ, is rehearsed across the letter. When Paul says that the gospel is for "the Jew first and also to the Greek," he implies that the gospel is not for the Greek instead of the Jew (1:16). The whole premise behind Romans 1:18–3:20 is that Jews and gentiles both stand condemned before God for their transgression. There is "no distinction" since Jews and gentiles have both sinned (3:22–23). On the flip side, there is "no distinction between Jew and Greek" in God's saving action in Christ because "one believes with the heart and so is justified, and one confesses with the mouth and so is saved," and "the same Lord is Lord of all and is generous to all who call on him" (10:10, 12). God is the God of Jews and gentiles and "he

---

2. Andrew Perriman, "What's Wrong with the 'Romans Road' to Salvation?," May 25, 2012, http://www.postost.net/2012/05/what-s-wrong-romans-road-salvation.

will justify the circumcised on the ground of faith and the uncircumcised through that same faith" (3:30). Paul describes Abraham as the forefather of all believers, whether Jewish or gentile, since God's "purpose was to make him the ancestor of all who believe without being circumcised and who thus have righteousness reckoned to them, and likewise the ancestor of the circumcised who are not only circumcised but who also follow the example of the faith that our ancestor Abraham had before he was circumcised" (4:11–12).

I need to stress that this is not unity as an abstract idea; this is unity for those who live a tenuous existence in the tenement house churches in Rome, where disease, destitution, and death are only ever a few hours away. This is unity where Christians, both Jews and gentiles, have received a hostile treatment from Roman synagogues for their messianic faith. This is unity amidst the expulsion and return of Jewish Christian leaders to the city of Rome in AD 49 and 54, which undoubtedly affected the social dynamics in the Roman churches in the interim (see Acts 18:1–2). This is unity in a context where it would have been easy for Christian gentiles to imbibe and replicate the anti-Jewish ethos of Roman elites who despised the Jews for being distinctive, different, insulated, and separated from wider society. This is unity when there was dispute and difference as to whether the regulations of the torah remained incumbent on all believers. This is unity at a time when the Roman churches could potentially fragment either along ethnic lines or according to divisions over torah observance.

This is why the climax of the letter, the summit of Paul's exhortation, is Romans 15:7–9: "Welcome one another, therefore, just as Christ has welcomed you, for the glory of God. For I tell you that Christ has become a servant of the circumcised on behalf of the truth of God in order that he might confirm the promises given to the patriarchs, and in order that the Gentiles might glorify God for his mercy." Paul's point here is that the Messiah came to serve the Jews, to make good the divine promises to Israel and to the patriarchs, so that Abraham might have a multiethnic family united in faith. The end result is that the gentiles would actually get saved, glorify God for his mercy, and obtain the obedience of faith. Accordingly, if the Messiah has welcomed Jews and gentiles into the family of Abraham, drawn them into God's electing purposes, made them members of his own body, the church, then they must welcome one another!

What Does This Church Look Like Today?

What does this kind of church look like today? Well imagine if a small church, either in the inner city or perhaps in a rural town, had an influx of Christian refugees from Syria and Sudan. Imagine if they came to this church, to your church, with their strange language, their recent experience of trauma, with strange ideas about worship, peculiar customs, personal complaints about things like having a US flag in the church, or an insistence that the minister should wear robes. Would you segregate them? Let them worship by themselves in the church hall after the main service with all the nice normal American folks? Even worse, what happens if more and more refugees arrive and take out membership, and suddenly you've got all these Syrians and Sudanese becoming the majority? You are only one congregational vote from changing your name from Fifth Baptist Church to St. John Chrysostom Community Church!

Well, this is what Romans is about! This is where you have to figure out how to "pursue what makes for peace and for mutual upbuilding" (14:19), discern how "each of us must please our neighbor for the good purpose of building up the neighbor" (15:2), and above all consider how you can live in "harmony with one another, in accordance with Christ Jesus, so that together you may with one voice glorify the God and Father of our Lord Jesus Christ" (15:5–6).

Rather than allowing our churches to be tribally divided, ghettocized by race or class, Paul's vision in Romans is for the lordship of Jesus Christ to be expressed in a physical expression of unity, amidst ethnic diversity and theological differences, so that everyone might glorify God for his mercy. Paul's Letter to the Romans tell us a lot about salvation, but it is principally about how the saved, Jews and gentiles, Americans and Arabs, Africans and Latinos, are drawn closer together as they are drawn closer to Jesus Christ.

6

God Justifies the Ungodly: Romans 4:1–8

Thomas R. Schreiner

The great Baptist preacher Charles Spurgeon tells the story of an artist who wanted to paint an unkempt and grubby street sweeper, but the street sweeper cleaned up for the painting because he didn't want to be painted in his dirty clothes. The painter sent him away because he wanted to paint the man as he truly was. Spurgeon points out that many of us are like that when it comes to the gospel. We think we will be acceptable to God if we clean ourselves up first before we come to him. We think that we can't come as we are to be saved. But God invites us to come just as we are, to admit our uncleanness, and to invite the Lord to clean us up. For God justifies the ungodly. God justifies the wicked. God justifies the unclean. That is the theme of our verses today, some of my favorite verses in the Bible. Let's read the verses.

> What then shall we say was gained by Abraham, our forefather according to the flesh? For if Abraham was justified by works, he has something to boast about, but not before God. For what does the Scripture say? "Abraham believed God, and it was counted to him as righteousness." Now to the one who works, his wages are not counted as a gift but as his due. And to the one who does not work but believes in him who justifies the ungodly, his faith is counted as righteousness, just as David also speaks of the blessing of the one to whom God counts righteousness apart from works:
> "Blessed are those whose lawless deeds are forgiven,
>   and whose sins are covered;
> blessed is the man against whom the Lord will not count his sin."
> (Rom. 4:1–8)[1]

---

1. Scripture quotations are from the ESV.

Justified by Faith

Paul has just argued in Romans 3 that we are justified by faith, not by the works of the law, which means that God as the divine judge declares us to be righteous in his sight, not guilty before him, if we trust in the death of Jesus to save us. Now he asks a vital question in chapter 4. Was Abraham justified by faith? After all, Abraham was the father of the Jewish people. Paul's Jewish opponents would have almost certainly brought up Abraham to defend the view that justification is by works. In fact, we have many references to Abraham in Jewish literature written after the close of the New Testament. And these writings emphasize Abraham's obedience. One Jewish writer says that Abraham was perfect in obeying the law (*Jubilees* 23:10). Again and again these Jewish writers point to Abraham's sacrifice of Isaac to show how amazing his works were, and thus it seems that many Jews believed that Abraham was justified by works, that he was right with God based on what he did. So, Paul says, let's take up the case of Abraham. Let's see what's the case with the forefather of the Jewish people.

We read in verse 2, "For if Abraham was justified by works, he has something to boast about."

Now this is obviously true, isn't it? If Abraham did the good works God required, then he would be justified before God by virtue of his works. And then Abraham could boast that his good works are what saved him. In verse 4 Paul gives an illustration so we understand what he is talking about in verse 2. "Now to the one who works, his wages are not counted as a gift but as his due." Paul gives an illustration from everyday life by considering the situation of an employee. And what Paul says here fits with common sense and everyday life. If you work for someone and he pays you, your salary is not a gift but an obligation. Your employer owes you the money since you worked for him.

In fact, if an employer doesn't pay you, he may be sued. At the very least you will be angry at him for not paying you, for you deserve to be compensated for the work you did. You may say thanks to your employer for employing you, but you rightly think that you deserve your paycheck. You worked for it, after all.

I worked eleven summers, from middle school through college, forty to sixty hours a week. I worked hard and made enough money to put me through college. And you know what? I never thanked anyone for my paycheck. I always thought I deserved it. That's what Paul is saying here. If Abraham was saved by his works, then he could boast of the things he did.

Abraham and Works

Then comes the most astonishing news. Paul makes it very clear that Abraham was not justified by works. Let's read verse 2 again. "For if Abraham was justified by works, he has something to boast about, but not before God." Note what Paul says at the end of the verse. Abraham could not boast before God. Now here is the key question. Why couldn't Abraham boast before God?

The answer is simple and clear. He couldn't boast before God because he didn't do the required good works. Abraham was a sinner who failed to do God's will. God only justifies those who obey him perfectly, and Abraham failed to do what God required (Gal. 3:10). And we all fail to obey God perfectly, which is the standard for salvation. Abraham lied about Sarah being his wife twice and put her in an abusive situation, and he wrongly had a child by Hagar his maidservant as well.

Verse 3 explains how Abraham was righteous before God. "For what does the Scripture say? 'Abraham believed God, and it was counted to him as righteousness.'" Paul quotes Genesis 15:6. We need to investigate the context of this verse. In Genesis 12 God promised Abraham land, children, and blessing, but when Genesis 15 rolls around, Abraham still doesn't have any children. And Abraham is discouraged since God's promise was not becoming a reality. Abraham says to the Lord, "I guess what you meant by your promise is that my servant Eliezer will be my heir." The Lord replies, "No. That is not my promise. Your very own son will be your heir." It was apparently a clear and beautiful night, and the Lord said to Abraham, "Go outside and look up at the sky. Count the stars." Obviously, they were too numerous to count. And the Lord said to Abraham, "So too your children will be uncountable." Abraham was an old man when this promise was made, and he could have said, "What? That can't be. I don't even have one child, so my offspring can hardly be as uncountable as the stars." But instead a miracle took place in Abraham's heart. He believed what God said.

Notice that faith doesn't just believe in anything. Faith trusts what God has revealed in his word, in the Scriptures. Somebody might tell you that they have faith that they will never get sick, but that is not biblical faith, since God never promises that. Faith is always tied to the promises of God.

Whatever you are going through, there are promises of God for you to cling to. When you read the Scriptures, look for God's promises and ask him to give you faith to believe them. One of the greatest promises is that God will be with us and strengthen us in every situation. So, what is the point so far? Abraham was right before God not because of his works but because of his faith. It was his faith that was counted as righteousness.

Verse 5 unpacks what Paul means. This is truly one of the most astonishing verses of the Bible. You might mention this verse when talking to unbelievers and just say, "Do you know what the Bible says?" and quote this verse. Consider how shocking and counterintuitive it is. "And to the one who does not work but believes in him who justifies the ungodly, his faith is counted as righteousness." Who is counted as righteous according to this verse? It is the one who does not work! It is those who are ungodly!

Ask the ordinary person who is right before God, and they will say it is the person who works hard at being obedient. But Paul says it is the one who doesn't work who is in the right before him. It is the one who doesn't try to impress God with the good things he or she has done. It is not the one who works who is right before God, but the one who believes, the one who trusts. And what does he or she trust? They trust that God justifies the ungodly through the work of Jesus Christ on the cross.

Do you see what Paul is doing here? He is putting Abraham in the company of the ungodly.

We read about Abraham in Joshua 24:2: "Long ago, your fathers lived beyond the Euphrates, Terah, the father of Abraham and of Nahor; and they served other gods." Before Abraham was saved, he was an idolater. Abraham was not a good person who was rewarded by God. Recently I read a blog post by a pastor named Mike McKinley warning us about the danger of subtly communicating to unbelievers our self-righteousness. We want unbelievers to know that we are sinners saved by Christ. We don't want to communicate to them rules we might follow, such as we don't watch television or we don't go to public schools or we don't listen to a particular kind of music or whatever our rule is. We may have good reasons for decisions like that, but those things are not the center of the gospel and should not be the message we communicate to the world. Jesus did not come to call the righteous but sinners to repentance. The gospel casts down our pride so that we can be lifted up by God's grace.

David and Forgiveness

We see the same truth in the life of David. David is also put in the company of the ungodly. "David also speaks of the blessing of the one to whom God counts righteousness apart from works: 'Blessed are those whose lawless deeds are forgiven, and whose sins are covered; blessed is the man against whom the Lord will not count his sin'" (Rom. 4:6–8). Paul quotes from Psalm 32 here.

In this psalm David confesses his sins and is surely thinking especially of his adultery with Bathsheba and his murder of Uriah. Notice how Paul introduces the quotation, referring to the blessing and joy of being counted righteous apart from works.

David focuses on forgiveness of sins. What a joy and blessing it is to have our lawless deeds forgiven, so that they are no longer held against us. Our sins are covered: they are put as far away from us as the east is from the west. The Lord doesn't count our sins against us anymore. Our friends and enemies may remember our sins, even after they say they have forgiven us, and bring them up against us again. That can happen even as a married couple, can't it? We can say we forgive, and then when we get angry with a person, we bring up their sin that we said we forgave. But God isn't like that. As Micah 7:19 says, he has cast our sins into the deepest sea and doesn't remember them anymore. We are free. I like what I heard Corrie Ten Boom say about this verse. God has thrown our sin into the deepest sea and put up a sign that says: No fishing!

On the day of judgment God will not say to us, "What about your sins?" He will say, "You are my beloved son and daughter. Enter into the joy of your master."

Are you carrying guilt around that you shouldn't be carrying? That guilt has been put on Jesus as the Son of God. And you are free from it. It is like growing up very poor. You are always reminded of how poor you are, and so you feel inferior to those who are rich. You are embarrassed about the house you live in and the clothes you wear and the car you drive. But now you have come into an inheritance. Suddenly you are rich, and those riches have been given to you. You did not earn the inheritance, and it is easy to forget you are rich since you were poor by birth and by nature. That is what it is like for us as sinners. We are poor before God by nature, but now we are rich because of the forgiveness of our sins. How easy it is to forget the riches that are ours in Jesus Christ. How easy it is to keep thinking that we are poor when we are now rich before him. We are God's beloved children through Christ.

Faith and Righteousness

Now I want to ask one final question from this text. When Paul says that faith is counted as righteousness, what does he mean?

Does he mean that faith *is* our righteousness? Is faith like a work that makes us righteous? Does faith itself save us? The answer to all these questions is no.

Faith in and of itself doesn't save us. Faith saves, as Romans 3:21–26 makes clear, because it unites us to Christ, who is our righteousness. Our righteousness comes from being united to Christ, so that Christ's righteousness is imputed to us.

We do not only receive forgiveness of sins; we also receive Christ's perfect obedience on our behalf—his righteous life. Faith saves because it connects us to Christ. Faith is the instrument or means of our justification, but not the ground. It is like the cord that plugs in an electric device, say a lamp. The power doesn't come from the cord but comes from electricity. The cord plugged into the wall connects to the electricity, and the electricity flows through the cord. No one would ever say that the power comes from the cord. The power flows through the cord. The cord is the instrument through which electricity flows. Faith is like the cord that connects to the electricity. It is the instrument by which Christ's righteousness is given to us. And even faith is given to us, as Ephesians 2:8 teaches us. Faith itself is a gift of God.

So we can't boast of anything. We depend entirely on Christ's righteousness for our salvation. We are naked, but we have come to him for dress. We are poor, but we have come to him for riches. We are miserable, but we have come to him for joy. We are ungodly, but we are righteous in Christ. Praise the Lord!

7

The Transforming Reality of
Justification by Faith: Romans 5:1–5

Carl R. Trueman

What difference does a doctrine make? That is a question with which many Christians wrestle. When I'm dealing with a difficult co-worker or trying to cope with my children's bad behavior, where does doctrine fit in? And, to raise the stakes even higher, how does all this Christian teaching help me when I'm faced with life's most fundamental and darkest reality: the suffering and death that must inevitably come my way at some point.

Indeed, that surely connects with those who are not Christians as well. We live in a world that tries to keep death out of sight or distracts us from its seriousness by turning it into a bit of cartoonish entertainment in a movie or a TV show. But deep down inside, everyone knows that suffering and death comes for all. Sooner or later, life's ultimate question will demand of us an answer.

It is here that the doctrine of justification by grace through faith is absolutely vital for the Christian's daily life and long-term hope, as this passage in Paul's Letter to the Romans (5:1–5) makes clear. The doctrine is not just an abstraction or a legal fiction. It touches us at our deepest level.

Indeed, in these five verses Paul makes three important points: justification by grace through faith in Christ is our foundation for life; its results are peace in the present and hope for the future; and this completely transforms our understanding of, and response to, the slings and arrows of this present life, giving a purpose to our sufferings as they are subverted to our good.

The Foundation: Justified in Christ

Moving from his discussion of Abraham and the promise given to him as patriarch, Paul has just connected our salvation to the same faith principle, Romans 4:23–25. Now he points to the result of all this. Clothed in the perfect righteousness of Christ, the believer has gained direct access to salvation. Notice: the verb is past tense. This has been done. It is accomplished. And by faith it is now true of us. It is not a piece of wishful thinking or a pious aspiration. It is not something we need to work toward. It is done, once and for all. We are justified in Christ now and can never be more so. Elsewhere, in Colossians 2:11–14, Paul uses dramatic language to speak of what has already been accomplished in Christ and how we are, in a profound and true sense, already raised in Christ. The same is true here: Christ has accomplished salvation on our behalf, and we are now the beneficiaries of his powerful, gracious work on our behalf. That is a fact.

Should that make a difference? Well, should it make a difference to a prisoner, to be told that he has been pardoned? To the cancer patient, to be informed that she is cured? To the bankrupt, to be assured that all his debts have been paid by another? Of course it should. How much more, then, should the good news of forgiveness in Christ have an impact on us? To hear that deliverance is accomplished, completely accomplished, is surely the most profoundly liberating news that anyone can hear. Paul is not here offering a technique on how to be saved. He is pointing to the reality and finality of God's action in Christ.

The Result: Peace and Hope

The results of this good news are manifold, but Paul highlights two in particular.

First, he notes that the Christian has peace with God. Now, peace in Scripture is a deep and significant idea. It means the putting away of the enmity that exists between sinful men and women and God so that they might enjoy deep and confident fellowship. Now, in the death of Christ, God's wrath has been put away, and those identified with him by faith stand before God clothed in their Savior's righteousness.

This is a beautiful, comforting truth. A lifetime of failure to reach God's standard of righteousness, the futility of efforts to pull ourselves up by our bootstraps—these take a toll and lead ultimately either to a Pharisaic self-righteousness or to despair. Neither option ultimately gives us real peace. The former rests on the delusion that we are good enough in ourselves to stand before God's judgment seat. The latter by its very definition can only mean mental turmoil and agony.

But if Christ has done it all for us and we have received it all by trust in the promise, what a difference that makes! We are now free—liberated from the burden of trying to appease God ourselves. We see in Christ the love of God shown forth to us. To quote Luther, we come to understand that "the love of God does not find but creates that which is pleasing to it." We do not have to make ourselves lovely to God in order for him to love us. It is because God loves us and has acted in Christ to save us that we are made lovely in his sight. Our sin is dealt with. Peace is established. What a burden of care that lifts from our shoulders!

Furthermore, Paul indicates that now we have a hope that is character-ized by rejoicing: we know that the day of consummation is coming, we look forward to it, and we rejoice at the thought of the glory of God that that entails. And notice the importance of certainty here. It is because of Christ's completed work on our behalf that Paul can rejoice—that requires him to have no shadow of doubt about the outcome. Only the solid foun-dation of Christ's justifying work allows Paul to write with such effusive confidence.

And Paul points out that this comes merely by grasping the promise that is in Christ. We have peace with God through the person and work of the Lord Jesus. The enmity between sinful human beings and their God has been removed. Luther saw this as the foundation of the freedom of the Christian. Thus, freed from the need to do works to make ourselves acceptable to God, we are freed, not to do whatever takes our self-indulgent fancy, but rather to do acts of love and kindness toward our neighbors.

The Practical Transformation: Rejoicing in Suffering

Finally, Paul points to the complete transformation of perspective on our present life that this peace with God through Christ brings. Because we are justified before God in Christ, nothing in this world can undermine that. Its complete and finished nature means that life can now be lived in a very different way. Most dramatically, all the sufferings that the world, the flesh, and the devil can throw at us are forced to work for our benefit. They are utterly subverted in Christ. As Christ on the cross used death as the means to life via resurrection, so we can now see our suffering as the means by which God leads us to hope.

This is clear from verses 3–5, where Paul describes how suffering shapes our Christian character, not in terms of giving us the Stoical ability to sol-dier on whatever the circumstances. Rather, suffering leads us ultimately to the virtue of hope, that dynamic, forward-looking expectation of the great things to come. Paul, of course, has a deep, personal experience of this—hence his statement in 2 Corinthians 4:16–18 comparing his present sufferings to the weight of eternal glory. As we suffer in this life, two things happen: we become more consciously dependent on God's grace, and we look forward more and more to our final destination in the new heavens and the new earth. All suffering is painful at the time. But in Christ it is subverted for our good.

The power for this, though, is not merely the result of our own reflection on the reality of our justification. Indeed, the doctrine of justification is not simply about an objective truth that exists external to us; it also highlights the fact that the Spirit now seals within our hearts the truth of Christ's death and resurrection on our behalf. The Spirit empowers us, not in order that we might be justified, but because we are already justified. Spiritual power, true spiritual power, is that which we are given by the indwelling of the Spirit himself, and it is characterized by our response to suffering. Salvation is no legal fiction. It is a powerful, transformative reality.

Conclusion

Thus we see the glories of justification by faith: peace with God, joyful hope for the future, and a radically transformed attitude to suffering in this life. It is no wonder that Paul—and Luther after him—saw this as lying at the very heart not only of Christian proclamation but also of Christian life as a whole.

New Perspective

8

The Balance of Already/Not Yet: Romans 8:1–17

James D. G. Dunn

"Already/not yet": this is a phrase which for many years has summed up the balance or tension which I find particularly in Paul's discussion of the Christian life, not least in his letter to the believers in Rome, and especially in its central chapters.

Already

Consider what Paul says in the buildup to chapter 8:

> How can we who died to sin go on living in it? Do you not know that all of us who have been baptized into Christ Jesus were baptized into his death? Therefore we have been buried with him by baptism into death, so that, just as Christ was raised from the dead by the glory of the Father, so we too might walk in newness of life. (6:2–4)[1]

> You have died to the law through the body of Christ, so that you may belong to another, to him who has been raised from the dead in order that we may bear fruit for God. While we were living in the flesh, our sinful passions, aroused by the law, were at work in our members to bear fruit for death. But now we are discharged from the law, dead to that which held us captive, so that we are slaves not under the old written code but in the new life of the Spirit. (7:4–6)

And now he reaches his climax:

---

1. Scripture quotations are usually from the NRSV but the author sometimes gives his own translation.

There is therefore now no condemnation for those who are in Christ
Jesus. For the law of the Spirit of life in Christ Jesus has set you free
from the law of sin and of death. (8:1–2)

Note the powerful imagery of death and life, of conversion as a sharing
in Christ's death and his resurrection. Conversion being seen as liberation—liberation from the fearful combination of flesh, sin, and law. "Flesh"
denoting that human weakness, the frailty of body and mind, which suc-
cumbs again and again to selfish temptation. "Sin" denoting the power of
self-centeredness. And the "law," telling us what God wants, but "weakened
by the flesh" and not strong enough to counter the downward pull of fleshly
desire and ambition (8:3). As Paul had put it in chapter 7, the power of
sin had abused the law, stirring up the very desires which the law warned
against. It had captivated the human "I," so that Paul could not refrain from
crying out, "Wretched man that I am! Who will rescue me from this body
of death?" (7:24). His immediate answer was Jesus Christ and his Spirit.
"For God has done what the law, weakened by the flesh, could not do: by
sending his own Son in the likeness of sinful flesh, and to deal with sin, he
condemned sin in the flesh, so that the just requirement of the law might
be fulfilled in us, who walk not according to the flesh but according to the
Spirit" (8:3–4).

So Paul makes very clear that there are *two foundations of new life* for
the believer. The first is what God has done in Christ: he has dealt with sin
in effect by loading it on Christ. The imagery is that of the sin offering—the
sin of the people loaded on the goat who carried it away into the wilderness
(Lev. 16). So the death of Christ is equivalent to the goat bearing away the
people's sins. The second foundation is the action of the Spirit. "The law of
the Spirit of life in Christ Jesus has set you free from the law of sin and of
death" (8:2). The power of the Spirit is stronger than the power of sin. This
is why, particularly here, Paul places such emphasis on the gift of the Spirit.
Indeed, Paul defines the Christian precisely in terms of the Spirit. First in
negative terms: "Anyone who does not have the Spirit of Christ does not
belong to him" (8:9). And then in positive terms: "All who are led by the
Spirit of God are children of God" (8:14).

In short, Paul's understanding of what it means to be a Christian has
both an objective element and a subjective element. The objective: what
God has done *for* us, independent of us, *extra nos*, in the ministry and
death of Jesus. The subjective: what God has done *in* us, given to us, the
Spirit of Christ. The two are interdependent. As the transition from chap-

ter 7 to chapter 8 makes clear, it is the gift of the Spirit which brings to reality in the individual believer what Christ achieved in his death and resurrection.

Not Yet

It is a feature of these three central chapters in Paul's letter to Rome that he first expresses the key point before indicating its complexity. In chapter 6 he starts by affirming that believers have "died to sin" because they have been baptized into Christ's death. But he goes on to urge his readers to resist the power of sin and the weakness of the flesh. Similarly, in chapter 7 he starts by pointing out that if a believer's old self-centered nature has died, then he is no longer subject to the law, before confronting the problem that the law still stirs up desire for what it warns against. So here, in chapter 8, having stressed what has already been achieved on behalf of and in the believer, Paul goes on to face the reality that believers are still in the flesh, of the flesh. Since sin and death are the fearful alliance, the not-yetness of death means that sin still exercises attraction.

The reality is that the believer has *not* left the flesh behind. There is no possibility of sinless perfection in the here and now. It is entirely possible still to walk according to the flesh. Conversion does not mean that the tension between flesh and Spirit has been left behind. On the contrary, that tension has been enhanced. The gift of the Spirit does not end the moral antithesis between flesh and Spirit. The antithesis is sharpened. Paul does not spare his readers from the reality of their present condition: "we are debtors, *not* to the flesh, to live according to the flesh—for if you live according to the flesh, you will die" (8:12–13).

Not to be ignored is the fact that he says this to Christians!

The reality is that believers are still in the body, and so still subject to death. Despite 7:24–8:2 Paul is clear: even though "Christ is in you" and "the Spirit is life," nevertheless "the body is dead because of sin" (8:10); the new life will not be complete until the body has been resurrected (8:13). An even clearer statement is 2 Corinthians 4:16 and 5:1: "Even though our outer nature is wasting away, our inner nature is being renewed day by day. . . . For we know that if the earthly tent we now live in is destroyed, we have a building from God, a house not made with hands, eternal in the heavens."

The key to Paul's thought here is to see salvation not as a past event ("Have you been saved?") but as a process—a process to a future completion. So, for example: "Now that we have been justified by his blood, will we be saved through him from the wrath of God. For if while we were enemies, we were reconciled to God through the death of his Son, much more surely, having been reconciled, will we be saved by his life" (Rom. 5:9–10); "The message about the cross is foolishness to those who are perishing, but to us who are being saved it is the power of God" (1 Cor. 1:18). In 1 Thessalonians 5:8 it is notable that the armor of God includes "the breastplate of faith and love," but also the helmet which is "the *hope* of salvation."

Paul is clear that the process of salvation climaxes in the resurrection of the body. Hence Romans 8:11: "If the Spirit of him who raised Jesus from the dead dwells in you, he who raised Christ from the dead will give life to your mortal bodies also through his Spirit that dwells in you."

So we can see what Paul's answer would be to the question "Are you saved?" It would be neither "Yes" nor "No," but "Not yet."

Consequences

The consequences of the "already/not yet" gospel are substantial.

1. The *privileges* are noteworthy. The first is indicated by the phrase "in Christ." To repeat the opening words of chapter 8, "There is therefore now no condemnation for those who are in Christ Jesus. For the law of the Spirit of life in Christ Jesus has set you free from the law of sin and of death" (8:1–2). But not to be missed is the way Paul balances the "in Christ" phrase with the parallel phrase "Christ in you": "Anyone who does not have the Spirit of Christ does not belong to him. But if Christ is in you, though the body is dead because of sin, the Spirit is life because of righteousness" (8:9–10). Christians are "in-Christ-ians" or "Christ-in-ians"—two sides of the same coin.

The gift of the Spirit is another way of putting the same thing. "You did not receive a spirit of slavery to fall back into fear, but you have received a spirit of adoption" (8:15). The contrast is noteworthy. Not a spirit of slavery—as though the Christian life were a continuous series of rule-obeying, or else. To be led by the Spirit is not to be ruled by fear. It is rather to experience God as a loving Father—the Spirit as the spirit of childlike trust. "When we cry, 'Abba! Father!' it is that very Spirit bearing witness with our spirit that we are children of God" (8:15–16). And then the most striking privilege of all: "And if children, then heirs, heirs of God and"—almost unbelievably—"joint heirs with Christ" (8:17).

Not to be missed is the strong sense of assurance which Paul here expresses: the believer can claim to be not just a child of God, an heir of God, but also a joint heir with Christ. A passage like this makes it impossible to reduce Christian discipleship to simply believing, a kind of intellectual exercise. Belief includes that, of course. But Paul makes it clear that there was a strong element of *feeling* in the earliest Christian discipleship. This was something John Wesley rediscovered afresh when he had what is usually referred to as his "Aldersgate experience." As he recalls in his journal:

> In the evening I went very unwillingly to a society in Aldersgate Street, where one was reading Luther's Preface to the Epistle to the Romans. About a quarter before nine, while he was describing the change which God works in the heart through faith in Christ, I felt my heart strangely warmed. I felt I did trust in Christ, Christ alone for salvation, and an assurance was given me that he had taken away my sins, even mine, and saved me from the law of sin and death. (May 14, 1738)

2. Paul also makes clear that the privileges bring *responsibilities*. These are summed up in the exhortation to "walk according to the Spirit." How may "the just requirement of the law" be fulfilled? Certainly not by living in accordance with the flesh, but rather by walking "in accordance with the Spirit" (8:4). Those in Christ have the responsibility to walk in accordance with the Spirit. For that too is integral to Paul's definition of a Christian. "For all who are led by the Spirit of God are children of God" (8:14). It is interesting and important to note that Paul so defines the Christian: not just as having the Spirit (8:9), but also as being led by the Spirit—a significant and somewhat disquieting conclusion for those who think of the Christian life primarily in terms of belief or of ritual enacted.

Romans 8:4–8 has an equally important checklist on the contrast Paul is drawing. To "live according to the flesh" is to set the mind "on the things of the flesh." And "to set the mind on the flesh is death," since "the mind that is set on the flesh is hostile to God; it does not submit to God's law" and indeed "cannot please God." Examples of that mind-set come easily to us, evident in the business, relationships, and politics of everyday life. In contrast, "those who live according to the Spirit set their minds on the things of the Spirit." "To set the mind on the Spirit is life and peace."

Paul later makes it clear that integral to such living in accord with the Spirit is a matter also of spiritual discernment. "Do not be conformed to this world, but be transformed by the renewing of your minds, so that you may discern what is the will of God—what is good and acceptable and perfect" (12:2). He expresses the same thought later, in his prayer for the Philippians. "My prayer is that your love may overflow more and more with knowledge and full insight to help you determine what is best, so that in the day of Christ you may be pure and blameless" (Phil. 1:9–10).

In Romans 8 Paul sums up the contrast between, on the one hand, a life lived to gratify self-centered desires and, on the other, a life lived enabled by the Spirit. "If you live according to the flesh, you will die; but if by the Spirit you put to death the deeds of the body, you will live" (8:13). The contrast is stark. The responsibilities are clear, as is the enabling from God—life in accordance with the Spirit of God and enabled by the strength the Spirit gives.

3. Finally, this key passage in Paul's theology sees the Christian life as a process of sharing in Christ's death as well as in his risen life. Romans 8:17 continues: "If children, then heirs, heirs of God and joint heirs with Christ—if, in fact, we suffer with him so that we may also be glorified with him." Note the "if," in Greek *eiper*, "provided that." Paul's clearest statement on the same theme is in Philippians 3:10–11: "I want to know Christ and the power of his resurrection and the sharing of his sufferings by becoming like him in his death, if somehow I may attain the resurrection from the dead."

Most striking is the order in which Paul sets out his hope to know Christ better. We might naturally expect Paul to put his shared experience with Christ in the sequence given by the climax to Jesus's own ministry—sharing in Christ's sufferings and becoming like him in his death, climaxed in experiencing the power of his resurrection. But no! Experiencing the power of Christ's resurrection is not the end of sharing in his sufferings. The new life from knowing Christ, the experience of the power of his resurrection, is not the end of the process. It is the beginning of the saving process. The sharing in Christ's sufferings is part of the life of discipleship. Becoming like him in his death is necessary if the old nature, the self-centered "I," is really to become like Christ. The beginning is only a beginning. It is the outworking of the resulting process, becoming like Christ, which proves its reality.

Conclusion

If Paul's gospel is to be properly understood, it is important to appreciate its twofold dimension marked by the "already/not yet" tension. Christ's death and resurrection were not the end of the story, but marked the beginning of the process of salvation, to be climaxed in his return. So the process of salvation in individual cases has a similar "already/not yet" tension—between what Christ has done and has still to do, between what Christ has begun in a believer's life and what he has still to do.

The tension can sometimes be depressing. Failure of one sort or another can be all too indicative of how much has yet to be done. So it is important that *both* are maintained—both the already *and* the not yet. To the despondent it is the already, what Christ has done, both on the cross and in their lives, which should be emphasized. To the overconfident, the casual or careless, it is the not yet which should be emphasized. Getting the balance right is the key to mature Christian living.

9

This Changes Everything: Romans 5:12–21

Tara Beth Leach

Signs and symptoms of sin and death are everywhere. They permeate our newsfeeds and news tickers. It's the mass shootings that plague our cities and communities. It's the explosions in the Middle East that rip apart families and take lives far too young. It's the hurting pastor seemingly eaten alive by his or her congregants. It's the family caught in the cycle of poverty for generations and generations and can't seem to dig themselves out. It's the child in another country with a distended stomach without access to a nutritious meal. It's the person in power who hurt or exploited the most vulnerable. It's the woman trapped as a sex slave with no possible way out. It's the "perfect" marriages that fall apart in the blink of an eye. It's friendships destroyed over meaningless drama. It's the life taken by cancer way too soon. Signs in every direction. The world is seemingly held hostage by sin, pain, death, and brokenness.

In the beginning, the shalom of God was settled on all of creation. As image bearers, Adam and Eve were in perfect harmony with God, one another, themselves, and creation.[1] But God's image bearers wandered from the plan, and almost immediately the world was fraught with difficulty. The tragic consequence is that the world is now severely out of joint. Not only is humanity seemingly burdened by sin, pain, death, and brokenness, but we consistently veer off from our intended identity as image bearers of God. We were created to reflect and imitate God, but we have wandered from that glorious design.

In times of trouble and chaos, humans respond in a variety of ways: (1) with despair—sometimes hopelessness is the go-to response; (2) with

---

1. Scot McKnight, *A Community Called Atonement*, Living Theology (Nashville: Abingdon, 2007), 21.

a fix-it-ourselves attitude—we live in a self-help, self-salvation world, and we work hard to create our own signs of hope through idolatry and consumerism; or (3) with callousness—if it's not happening in our own backyard or affecting us personally, it's easier to turn a blind eye. If despair, self-help, or callousness aren't the best responses, then what is? Is there *any* hope?

Earth-Shattering Word of Hope

In Romans 5:12–21, the apostle Paul returns to the origins of this diseased world and offers an earth-shattering word of hope.

> Therefore, just as sin entered the world through one man, and death through sin, and in this way death came to all people, because all sinned—
>
> To be sure, sin was in the world before the law was given, but sin is not charged against anyone's account where there is no law. Nevertheless, death reigned from the time of Adam to the time of Moses, even over those who did not sin by breaking a command, as did Adam, who is a pattern of the one to come.
>
> But the gift is not like the trespass. For if the many died by the trespass of the one man, how much more did God's grace and the gift that came by the grace of the one man, Jesus Christ, overflow to the many! Nor can the gift of God be compared with the result of one man's sin: The judgment followed one sin and brought condemnation, but the gift followed many trespasses and brought justification. For if, by the trespass of the one man, death reigned through that one man, how much more will those who receive God's abundant provision of grace and of the gift of righteousness reign in life through the one man, Jesus Christ!
>
> Consequently, just as one trespass resulted in condemnation for all people, so also one righteous act resulted in justification and life for all people. For just as through the disobedience of the one man the many were made sinners, so also through the obedience of the one man the many will be made righteous.
>
> The law was brought in so that the trespass might increase. But where sin increased, grace increased all the more, so that, just as sin

reigned in death, so also grace might reign through righteousness to bring eternal life through Jesus Christ our Lord. (NIV)

After returning to the origins of brokenness, Paul outlines the way in which the creator God has worked to restore the world and deal with the problem of sin, death, and brokenness. As Paul has outlined in previous chapters of Romans, especially Romans 1:18–32, he points out that humanity as a whole is held captive by sin. But now in addressing the problem of sin and evil, Paul gets to the root of the issue. In the beginning there was unity, trust, mutuality, vulnerability, perfect love without fear, and shalom. But then humanity rebelled against its creator God, and things took a tragic turn. Sin and evil's corrosive effects were noticeable almost immediately. In attempting to usurp the role of God and turning against one another, humanity experienced death, pain, division, disunity, violence, tears, domination, and oppression.

But as the story of God unfolds, we see that time and time again God moves in with an act of grace and a plan for redemption. God is not only the creator God but also the covenant God. God promises to make a great nation, a holy nation, and a light to the other nations. We see the salvific power of God as the Israelites are rescued from the grip of Egypt. In response to God's saving grace, the people of God are given the gift of the law. If they lived in the boundaries of this good and beautiful law, the world would be able to peer into the holy nation and see what God is like. However, as Paul notes, the problem of humanity's sin and brokenness was merely magnified through the law.

Yet God never pulled in the reins on faithfulness. As the story of God unfolds, God continues to deepen and expand God's promises until it culminates in the faithfulness of God in Christ. Born in the margins and with a death certificate in his hand, this divine King gives us a reason to not despair, as good news bursts forth into the world.

Overturned

The disaster of sin and evil in Adam is overturned by the faithfulness of King Jesus. In his faithfulness, he lived the life Adam couldn't live, lived the life Israel was intended to live, completed and fulfilled the perfect law of love and peace, embodied the perfect image of God, and taught and lived the countercultural ways of the kingdom of God. And on a dark day the looming death warrant was driven into his hands and feet, and the powers of sin, evil, shame, and decay were heaped on this king. The disobedience of the people of God was reversed, and the disaster of Israel was overturned in King Jesus. And now the powers that have hijacked our hearts and minds have been upended through the grace of God. The corrosive power of sin, decay, and death has been capsized.

This Changes Everything

This gift of God is presently bursting forth and restoring all of creation, washing over us even now with restorative power. This grace permeates even the most corroded hearts and broken systems and has the power to transform any and all who will receive it. Yes indeed, when we open our news feeds and walk out our doors, the death introduced in Adam characterizes this present age. But this does not mean we despair! It is because of the life, fulfillment of Scripture, death, resurrection, and exaltation of Jesus, the gift of the Spirit, and the birth of the church that life crashes into our world and should therefore characterize the people of God in Christ! This is the good news for us today as we gather: just as Christ offers a radical alternative to death, so should the people of God offer to the world a radical alternative that characterizes the world to come.

Adam Solidarity or Jesus Solidarity?

So, then, who or what will we characterize? Will we live in Adam solidarity or will we live in Jesus solidarity?[2] If you aren't sure, allow me to illustrate the two:

Adam solidarity: driven to sacrifice others for my gain
Jesus solidarity: driven to sacrifice oneself for the sake of another

---

2. "Adam solidarity" and "Jesus solidarity" are terms used by James Dunn in his commentary on Romans. James D. G. Dunn, *Romans*, 2 vols., Word Biblical Commentary, 38a and 38b (Grand Rapids: Zondervan, 2015), 288–399.

Adam solidarity: driven to turn a blind eye to structural evil that hurts
the poor and vulnerable
Jesus solidarity: driven to overturn structural evil in this world through
the power of the Holy Spirit

Adam solidarity: driven to talk merely about God
Jesus solidarity: driven to talk to God

Adam solidarity: driven to meet my desires above all else
Jesus solidarity: driven to meet others' needs

Adam solidarity: driven to usurp the role of God by seeking fame, honor,
and power
Jesus solidarity: driven to submit to the reign and rule of Jesus and see
his radically countercultural kingdom unleashed in the world

Adam solidarity: driven to endless consumption—bigger, better, more,
shinier
Jesus solidarity: driven to sacrifice

Adam solidarity: driven to divide and build barriers
Jesus solidarity: driven to be a bridge builder by bringing unity where
there is division, and reconciliation where there are barriers

Adam solidarity: driven to love only when it's convenient
Jesus solidarity: driven to love even when it hurts

Adam solidarity: driven to harbor bitterness
Jesus solidarity: driven to grace and forgiveness

Adam solidarity: driven to negativity and despair
Jesus solidarity: driven to hope

Adam solidarity: driven to bringing others down
Jesus solidarity: driven to lift others up and proclaim the life-changing
power of Jesus

You see, dear ones, the grace of God has reached into the kingdom of sin, corrosion, and decay and delivers those of us who are held captive. But it isn't just about rescue, no; we are propelled and impelled by this grace to live the way of life, love, and grace. And by doing so, we are offering the world a very radical alternative. We no longer need to live the way of sin and death! All who are in Christ have left the old solidarity and belong to the new; therefore, we embody the cruciform life of Jesus today. Which solidarity do you stand in?

It Begins and Continues with Yes

On a strangely warm January evening in Upstate New York, my then boy-friend asked me if I would join him on a sunset date for hot chocolate on a bench overlooking the picturesque town of Owego. It was an evening to remember as we sat there on the bench, slowly sipping from our to-go mugs and enjoying one another's presence. Just as the sun was about to disappear from the horizon, my boyfriend, Jeff, handed me a card. I opened the card and read his reflections on our relationship together. At the end of the card he wrote, "So I have just one question for you . . ." When I looked up, Jeff was on one knee with a ring in his hand. "Tara Beth, will you marry me?" "Yes, yes, yes!" I exclaimed.

That passionate yes on that strangely warm January evening set the trajectory for the rest of my life. It was a life-changing yes; it was a yes so strong that it then became a no to anything that would ever come between me and Jeff. God wants your yes. God wants your life-changing, life-transforming yes; the type of yes that will set the trajectory for the rest of your life; the type of yes that is so strong that it's a no to the old solidarity.

It is because of God's grand yes to us that the grace of God meets us exactly where we are. We don't have to earn it, and we don't have to change first to receive it. The invitation is a simple, life-altering yes. God wants your moment-by-moment, minute-by-minute, second-by-second, breath-by-breath, step-by-step, situation-by-situation *yes*. He wants your naked vulnerability, your heart. A yes to God's way, to the Jesus life, to God's future, to God's plan, to God's shalom, to God's leading, to God's visions, to God's aches for the world, to God's empowering, and to God's calling.

It is when we, the bride of Christ, say yes to God that we show the world a radical alternative way of living.

In closing, dear ones, I invite you to stand and join me in this responsive reading. I invite you to stand in a posture of surrender—with your hands out and your palms open.

Pastor: Dear God, we say yes to you moment by moment, minute by minute, second by second, step by step, breath by breath, situation by situation, relationship by relationship, job by job, day by day, and longing by longing.
Congregation: Yes, God.

P: Yes. Yes to you and your way.
C: Yes, God.

P: Your future.
C: Yes, God.

P: Your shalom.
C: Yes, God.

P: Your leading.
C: Yes, God.

P: Your visions.
C: Yes, God.

P: Your aches for the world.
C: Yes, God.

P: Your empowering.
C: Yes, God.

P: Your emboldening.
C: Yes, God.

P: Your calling.
C: Yes, God.

P: Yes to all of you. All of your leading. All of your ways. Moment by moment, minute by minute, second by second, step by step, breath by breath, situation by situation, relationship by relationship, job by job, day by day, longing by longing.
C: Yes, God. Amen.

10

Pass the Peace by Faith: Romans 4:1–4, 13–17

Scot McKnight

In a few minutes each of us will "pass the peace" to one another to extend the peace of God that has been "passed on" to us. By then we have listened to the readings from Scripture and this theological and narrowly focused homily, which will be set in the context of our faith by confessing the Apostles' Creed. We will then pray together and confess our sins, and then Jay will give the absolution. And *only then* will be able to pass the peace of the Lord on to others.

The Passing of the Peace

There's a glorious theological order in an Anglican liturgy. (Can I get a witness?) The passing of the peace comes at the crucial point in our time of worship when we are all reconciled with God through confession and forgiveness, when we are ready to pass that divine grace of reconciliation on to others, and all this so we will all be ready (as we can be) for Eucharist. It is not hard for us to imagine from our reading of Romans that Paul has in mind the Strong and Weak in our congregations who need to welcome one another.

Peace, you know, cannot be taken for granted.

Nor should it be passed on carelessly or lightly or meaninglessly.

Goodness, if we think about it too hard, we will realize we are passing on the good news of redemption—we are passing on the peace of the Lord to all those in our fellowship as we say "The peace of Christ" to one another.

I will say this more forcefully: the most demanding element of the service this morning is passing the peace. It may be the most hypocritical

---

Lectionary Readings for Sunday: Year A, Lent 2: Genesis 12:1–4; Psalm 121; Romans 4:1–5, 13–17; John 3:1–17.

moment or it may be the most honest moment of the morning. It is hypocritical because it is demanding congruence between what we say and what we are (reconciled with God and with one another), and we may not always be in a state of congruence. Passing the peace's honesty turns our words into an act of grace that God pulses through us to others. (Of course, we don't need the Book of Common Prayer to tell us that reconciliation with God and others is the will of God: it is, after all, the vision of God for the church.)

Why say this? Why ruin a perfectly wonderful, innocent little element of our liturgy? Why complicate what ain't so? Because peace between God and humans and between each of us is a gospel achievement, a kingdom reality in the church.

Peace is a miracle, an act of grace, and part of new creation.

Far easier to say peace than to indwell that peace.

The readings from Scripture point the way to indwell the peace that we pass.

You will have noticed that we dipped into God's promise to Abram to make him a great nation, a promise Abram accepted by faith (three chapters later). God's promise in Genesis 12 led to reading a psalm that reminds us that our help comes from a loving, watching, protecting God. And these texts were met by two powerful giants—Paul in Romans 4 reminding us that Abraham was made right with God on the basis of faith, and then Jesus's beautiful image in John 3 that faith—or believing—creates a new birth, a birth from above.

We don't often go to the epistle reading for our sermons, so I shall this morning. I want to because of a question we need to consider.

A Historical Question

My question: What was it like for the churches of the apostle Paul—like the church in Rome—to "pass the peace"? History alert: no, they probably did not use the Book of Common Prayer and bang knees against pews when they were passing the peace. But Paul cared about peace, and so it's a fair question. What was it like to pass the peace in the Pauline churches? What did it take for them to indwell the peace? What was it like for the two opposing parties in the Roman churches, the Strong and the Weak as we read in chapters 14–15, to pass the peace? Did they? Did they want to?

I begin then with a history lesson, one I learned from Peter Oakes in his book *Reading Romans in Pompeii*. Oakes asked a simple question: If Paul's churches were based on the space of a typical "house" in Pompeii, who would be in that space? Who would be at the house? Then Oakes fiddled with numbers and figured out what the same typical house church would look like in Rome and in others of Paul's churches. Let's remember that Paul's churches did not meet in church buildings but in houses. Not houses like our suburban homes, but walled and roofed entire blocks with irregular walls inside that block. Entering into a set of homes in Rome would be a bit like entering into an indoor flea market with irregular-sized shops but somehow finding pathways through the whole.

Who would have been there? Here is what Oakes discovered—and once we see this, we discover that "passing the peace" was a challenge. There would be thirty people in total, comprising

- a craftworker who rents a workshop with separate living accommodation for his family and some male slaves, a female domestic slave, and a dependent relative;
- a few other householders who rent less space, with family and slaves and dependents;
- a couple of members of families whose householder is not part of the house church;
- a couple slaves whose owners are not part of the house church;
- a couple of free or freed dependents of people who are not part of the house church;
- a couple of homeless people;
- a few people who are renting space in shared rooms (migrant workers, etc.).

Now let's get more realistic. If any of the slaves was a woman—and yes, there were Roman female slaves in Paul's churches—it would be not at all unlikely, in fact quite certain, that her services would be under the control of her owner, and if she was a slave girl at an inn, his guests would have paid for her services. I'm speaking here, of course, of her body. *And she could do nothing about it.* She was a slave, she was owned.

Pass the peace, indeed. And pray for her in doing so, and pray she will be set free.

Now let's ramp this up to another level. Add some Jewish believers who eat kosher and who are torah observant and who are now doubly nervous about this strange fellowship Paul is creating. "The Weak" is the term Paul uses for them at Rome. "What," Schlomo asks himself, "if my son Schmuley chooses to marry that Roman slave's daughter, Dora?"

Pass the peace, indeed. And pray gentiles will become torah observant. Or pass the peace and the gentiles can pray the Jews will give up their non-Roman ways.

In the midst of this we hear echoing off the walls of the Roman house church words from Paul from the beginning and end of his ministry, words that shaped his prayers and everything he taught.

> There is no longer Jew or Greek, there is no longer slave or free, there is no longer male and female; for all of you are one in Christ Jesus. (Gal. 3:28)[1]

> In that renewal there is no longer Greek and Jew, circumcised and uncircumcised, barbarian, Scythian, slave and free; but Christ is all and in all! (Col. 3:11)

Pass the peace, indeed. To all, to everyone, to Jew and to Greek and to males and to females, to slaves and to the free, to barbarians and Scythians.

Because Christ Has Made Them One

The question is why. Why pass the peace?

The answer is because Christ has made them one. He has sent his mighty peace into their midst to create peace between those who were never together.

Pass the peace. To one and all.

Before we turn to Romans 4 to see how the peace can be achieved as we pass it on, I want to use an analogy of what Paul envisions for his churches. There are three ways to eat (or make) a salad.

1. Gather your ingredients and scatter them into separate bowls.
2. Gather your ingredients, mix them, and then smother them with salad dressing.
3. Gather your ingredients, mix them, and then drizzle some extra virgin olive oil to enhance the flavor of each ingredient.

1. Scripture quotations are from the NRSV.

The first is the way of Sunday-morning churches in America: each different group of people—African Americans, Latin Americans, Irish Americans, Italian Americans, English Americans, Scottish Americans—gathers into a separate church. Or Baptists and Presbyterians and Catholics and Lutherans and Evangelical Free and Covenant and Orthodox—all gathered into separate churches. Anglicans, of course, are not responsible for church divisions.

The second is the way of America's past: mix everyone together *but smother them all with a single taste so everything tastes the same.* To change metaphors, this is Penguin Christianity where we all look alike and waddle alike. Back to the salad dressing smothering, this sort of Christianity *pretends* to like diversity but doesn't know what it really is. It instead *colonizes* all diversity into coerced uniformity. Yes, that means white cultural Protestant Christianity.

The third is Paul's mission and Paul's vision: mix everyone together, let each person be who she or he is, let each group throb with its natural diversity, but let's all sit at the table and indwell the unity we have in Christ. Let's dance. Let's not offend the conscience of our sister or brother by coercing uniformity. And let's enjoy the freedom of the Spirit as each grows into maturity.

Yes, that's the challenge of the church that Paul's mission took on: bringing gentiles into the people of God that was formerly designed only for spinach leaves—Jews. Paul has mixed arugula, chard, fruits and nuts, tomatoes, carrots, and Pecorino Romano cheese into the spinach leaves. For Paul, to pass the peace meant to *welcome the unwelcomed, to embrace the unembraced, and to dine with the uninvited.* For him it meant the Strong would create welcome for the Weak, and the Weak would not look down on the Strong for eating pork.

Passing the peace, indeed, was Paul's biggest challenge. The mission God gave to Paul was to bring gentiles into the old family of God—to make the spinach leaves vibrate with the discomfort of new neighbors in the salad bowl.

Passing the Peace by Faith

How can we pass the peace and achieve the peace of reconciliation? Paul tells us. To see how we can do this we turn to Romans 4:1–4, 13–17, our epistle reading from this morning.

What then are we to say was gained by Abraham, our ancestor according to the flesh? For if Abraham was justified by works, he has something to boast about, but not before God. For what does the scripture say? "Abraham believed God, and it was reckoned to him as righteousness." Now to one who works, wages are not reckoned as a gift but as something due. . . .

For the promise that he would inherit the world did not come to Abraham or to his descendants through the law but through the righteousness of faith. If it is the adherents of the law who are to be the heirs, faith is null and the promise is void. For the law brings wrath; but where there is no law, neither is there violation.

For this reason it depends on faith, in order that the promise may rest on grace and be guaranteed to all his descendants, not only to the adherents of the law but also to those who share the faith of Abraham (for he is the father of all of us, as it is written, "I have made you the father of many nations")—in the presence of the God in whom he believed, who gives life to the dead and calls into existence the things that do not exist.

First, Abraham was made right with God *by faith* and not by works of the law, those works that made Jews separate from gentiles. Second, the law is a Moses thing. Faith is an Abraham thing. Justification occurred before Moses because Abraham was justified by faith. The ground of our acceptance with God is faith; the ground of our union with Christ is faith. Third, because it is by faith and not the works of the law, justification is not just for Jews but also for gentiles.

Acceptance with God is based on faith.

Peace with God is based on faith.

We *pass the peace* by faith.

What Paul is saying here is that gentiles don't have to become Jews to be accepted by God. What he is saying is that women don't have to become men. Slaves don't have to become free. Scythians don't have to become Jews, and barbarians don't have to put away their Minnesota Vikings helmets and move to Illinois. Because they are accepted by God on the basis of faith, they are accepted; whom God accepts is accepted. Whom God accepts we are to accept.

Pass the peace, indeed. We are now called to pass the peace to all. We are called to mix it up in the salad bowl in such a way that the flavor of each rises to the surface, each person has a distinct flavor in our fellowship. We are to know that there are males and females here and that's good; we are to know there are some singers and some non-singers; we are to know there are some employed and some unemployed.

So here's Paul's theory of passing the peace: *we can only truly pass the peace by faith.* Not because we have earned it with God or with one another; not because some of us are more worthy of the peace than others. We pass the peace by faith because by faith God has spread his peace to us.

Passing the Peace to All

But sometimes some of us are invisible, as in Ralph Ellison's *Invisible Man.* I will now begin to probe those who tend to go unnoticed in our churches.

Widows. *Invisible?*

Listen to how Miriam Neff, a widow, tells her story:

> I am part of the fastest growing demographic in the United States. We are targeted by new-home builders and surveyed by designers. We are a lucrative niche for health and beauty products, and financial planners invite us to dinners. It's no wonder the marketers are after us: 800,000 join our ranks every year.
>
> Who are we? We are the invisible among you—the widows.
>
> Studies show that widows lose 75 percent of their friendship network when they lose a spouse. Sixty percent of us experience serious health issues in that first year. One third of us meet the criteria for clinical depression in the first month after our spouse's death, and half of us remain clinically depressed a year later. Most experience financial decline. One pastor described us by saying we move from the front row of the church to the back, and then out the door. We move from serving and singing in choir to solitude and silent sobbing, and then on to find a place where we belong.[2]

Who else might go unnoticed in our churches?

Children. *Invisible?*

Teenagers. *Invisible?*

Seniors. *Invisible?*

2. Miriam Neff, "The Widow's Might," *Christianity Today,* January 18, 2008, http://www.christianitytoday.com/ct/2008/january/26.42.html.

Races. *Invisible?* Asian Americans are the fastest growing ethnic group in the USA, and 50 percent of Asian Americans profess faith in Christ. Our church area is filled with ethnic diversity—we enjoy one another's food more than one another's fellowship.

Women—those whom Carolyn Custis James calls "half the church," and she knows in some parts of the world it's way above 50 percent.[3] *Invisible?*

The poor. *Invisible?*

Those who have experienced tragedies. *Invisible?*

Faith strugglers. *Invisible?*

The non-university-educated. *Invisible?*

Introverts. *Invisible?* (Okay, they like it.)

The sexually abused. *Invisible?*

Those from dysfunctional families. *Invisible?*

The depressed. *Invisible?*

The anxious. *Invisible?*

I'll stop listing those to whom we are called to pass the peace in faith.

Passing the peace creates a level playing field if we indwell it by faith in Christ that re-creates us. The church is for all sorts of people who come for grace and who come for forgiveness and who come for love. Our church is not a church for the sanctified and perfected but for the unsanctified and the imperfect.

The church, and I'll end now, is God's space for peace. Peace with God and peace with our brothers and sisters in Christ—*all* our brothers and sisters. When we pass the peace, folks, we are extending the empowering grace of God to embrace others in the way God has embraced us. Extend your arms to one and all. Extend and embrace in faith.

May I suggest today that when we say "The peace of the Lord," we add "by faith" to it?

We can only achieve the peace of the blessing by faith.

---

3. Carolyn Custis James, *Half the Church: Recapturing God's Global Vision for Women* (Grand Rapids: Zondervan, 2010).

Apocalyptic Perspective

11

Immortal Combat: Romans 1:16–17 and 5:12–14

Jason Micheli

According to the *Washington Post* this week, the local Alexandria chapter of Washington Sport and Health just canceled the gym membership of Richard Spencer, the president of the alt-right, white nationalist National Policy Institute.

Spencer was pumping iron in safe anonymity, when C. Christine Fair, a Georgetown University professor, recognized him and then confronted him. At first he denied his identity. But she was sure it was him. According to the other patrons, the professor lambasted him, yelling, "Not only are you a Nazi—you are a cowardly Nazi." The gym canceled his membership after the altercation.

Reading the article, my first thought was: "That's what makes the church different than the gym."

I wouldn't disagree with the Georgetown professor's characterization of Richard Spencer as a repugnant, cowardly Nazi. I'd even go farther than her. I don't know Dr. Fair, but if she's a Christian, rather than agitate for his removal from a club, her first response to Richard Spencer should have been to invite him to the club we call "church."

Now, I'm *not* suggesting Richard Spencer is entitled to his noxious views, nor am I minimizing how monstrous they are. By any accounting Richard Spencer is racist. He's anti-Semitic. He's xenophobic. He's an "America first" idolator. He's likely homophobic and sexist too.

In response to getting booted from Washington Sport and Health, Spencer tweeted: "[Does this mean] we can start kicking Jews and coloreds out of our business establishments?"

Richard Spencer is ungodly. I can think of no one who fits the definition better.

And that's my problem. Because the apostle Paul says it's exactly someone like Richard Spencer for whom Christ died (Rom. 5:6).

If it was a gym to which we all belonged, then I'd be the first to say, "Kick him out on his a@#."

But we're not members of a club. We're members of a Body created by a particular kerygma: that on the law-cursed cross God in Jesus Christ died for the ungodly, that Christ's death defeated the Power of Death.

Christ didn't die to make nice people nicer. Christ died so that ungodly cretins might become a new creation. Richard Spencer is precisely the sort of ungodly person we should invite to church.

Where else could he go? *This is the only place where the Word of the Cross might vanquish him, delivering him from his bondage to the Power of Sin.*

I chose that last sentence with care. "Bondage to the Power of Sin," with a capital *P* and a capital *S*, is the only way to speak Christianly about Richard Spencer's racism; in fact, the Power of Sin with a capital *P* and a capital *S* is the only way to speak Christian.

Our text, Romans 5:6, is Paul's thesis statement, and from it he unwinds a single, nonlinear argument. The argument itself is odd.

From the Congregation to the Cosmic

Unlike Paul's other letters, this one continuously shifts focus from the congregation to the cosmic, as though what concerns this little house church in Rome somehow also concerns all of creation.

The letter is also odd in that Paul puts the salutations, along with the introduction of the main theme, not at the beginning of the letter but at the very end. The introduction of the main theme comes like a final reveal: "The God of peace will in due time crush the Power of Satan under your feet" (16:20).[1]

This is why Paul so often uses the language of combat and battle and powers and invasion. The theme of this whole letter is the defeat of the Power of Satan, and Paul's thesis is that the gospel is the Power by which God defeats that Power: "For I am not ashamed of the gospel. . . . For in it the righteousness of God is revealed" (1:16–17).

Trouble is, Paul's thesis statement doesn't sound like it's about the defeat of anything, much less the Power of Satan. This is because the English lan-

---

1. The translation is Beverly Roberts Gaventa's, in her book *When in Romans* (Grand Rapids: Baker Academic, 2016).

guage lacks any equivalents to the Greek word that gets translated throughout Romans as either "righteousness" or "justification."

In the Greek, *dikaiosynē* is a noun with the force of a verb; it creates that which it names. The only word in English that comes close to approximating *dikaiosynē* is *rectify/rectification*. So "righteousness" here isn't an attribute or adjective. It's a Power to bring salvation to pass. It's God's powerful activity to rectify what is wrong in the world.

And the way God is at work in the world is the gospel, the Word of the Cross. Through it, God's rectifying Power is revealed. In Greek it's *apokalyptetai*: apocalypse, invasion.

Literally, Paul says, "For I am not ashamed of the gospel, for in it the rectifying Power of God is invading . . ." Note the present tense.

You Can Only Invade Territory Held by an Enemy

If you think of sin as something you do, then you cannot understand what the Son of God came to do.

For as much as we think Christianity is about forgiveness, Paul doesn't use the word. Indeed, he uses the word "repent" only once.

Repenting is something we do. Paul's Letter to the Romans isn't at all about anything we do. It's everywhere about what God does.

It makes no sense to forgive slaves for their enslavement. Captives cannot repent their way out of bondage. Prisoners can only be delivered. From an enemy.

Only at the end of his long letter does Paul finally reveal this enemy as Satan.

In chapter 3 he names the enemy Sin with a capital *S* and calls it an alien, anti-god Power whose power we are all under and from whom we're unable to free ourselves (3:9).

In chapter 5 he makes Sin-with-a-capital-*S* synonymous with Death-with-a-capital-*D* (5:12).

In chapter 8 he widens the lens to show how it's not just us but all of creation that is held in captivity to the Power of Sin and Death (8:21).

And in chapter 13 he tells the Christians in Rome that they should put away the works of darkness and put on the "weapons of light" (13:12), which he also calls the "weapons of rectification" (6:13).

Finally, at the end he reveals the enemy as Satan from whose bonds only the invading righteousness of God can free us.

Inside the Church We've Not Remembered

Outside the church it's Memorial Day weekend, when we remember those who've fallen in war.

We've forgotten, such that this all probably sounds strange to you. We've forgotten that salvation itself is a battle. We've forgotten that God has a real enemy that God's determined to destroy.

We've forgotten that the cross of Jesus Christ is God's invasion from on high and that our proclamation of his act on the cross is itself the weapon by which the God of peace is even now rectifying a world where Satan still rules but his defeat is not in question.

Salvation isn't our evacuation from earth to God. Salvation is God's invasion of earth, in and through the cross of Jesus Christ, the Power that looks like no power.

Only when you understand Scripture's view of Sin as a Power and our sinfulness as bondage to it can you understand why and how Paul can claim something as repugnant as there being no distinction whatsoever between someone like you and someone like Richard Spencer (2:1).

That's not to say you're all as rotten as Richard Spencer; it's to say that all of us are captive, all of creation is captive, to a pharaoh called Sin.

And not one of us is safe from God's rectifying work.

To invite Richard Spencer to church, then, isn't to minimize or dismiss his noxious racism or odious views. It's to take them so seriously that you invite him to the only place where he might by assaulted by the only Word with the Power to vanquish him and create him anew.

During their confrontation at Washington Sport and Health, Dr. Fair, the Georgetown professor, yelled at Richard Spencer: "I find your presence in this gym to be unacceptable, your presence in this town to be unacceptable." The gym later terminated his membership without comment.

In all likelihood, inviting him to church would be as bad for our business as the management of the gym judged it to be bad for their business. Maybe "bad for business" is what Paul means by the scandal of the gospel.

You haven't really digested the offense of the gospel until you've swallowed the realization that it means someone like Richard Spencer might be sitting in the pew next to you, his hand out to pass the peace of Christ, the weapon which surpasses all understanding.

You haven't really comprehended the cosmic scope of God's salvation until you've realized it includes both you and Richard Spencer, both of you potential victims of the awful invading Power of the gospel of God's unconditional grace.

I haven't actually invited Richard Spencer to this church.

Yet.

But I did leave a copy of this sermon in the door of his townhouse yesterday.

I don't know that he'd ever show up.

But I do know—I'm not ashamed of it—that this gospel is powerful enough to defeat the Powers of the enemy that enslaves him.

In Celebration of Full Communion: Romans 3:21–24

Fleming Rutledge

But now the righteousness of God has been manifested apart from law, although the law and the prophets bear witness to it, the righteousness of God through faith in Jesus Christ for all who believe. For there is no distinction; since all have sinned and fall short of the glory of God, they are justified by his grace as a gift, through the redemption which is in Christ Jesus.

Romans 3:21–24[1]

The Glory of Baptism

In the context of this service in which we have just renewed our baptismal covenant, I greet you with these words of Martin Luther about what he calls "the glory of baptism":

Baptism is the prime sacrament, the foundation of them all. . . . There are two things which baptism signifies, namely, death and resurrection. . . . We call this death and resurrection a new creation, a regeneration, a spiritual birth. . . . The sacrament of baptism, even as a sign, is not a momentary action, but something permanent. While the rite itself is quite transitory, yet the purpose which it signifies lasts until death; indeed, till the Resurrection at the last day. . . . You must under-

---

1. Scripture quotations, unless otherwise indicated, are from the RSV.

A sermon in celebration of full communion for the Episcopal Church in the USA and the Evangelical Lutheran Church in America, preached at Trinity Episcopal Cathedral, Columbia, South Carolina, on the Feast of the Annunciation, March 25, 2001.

Dedicated to the memory of the Rev. Professor Edmund A. Steimle.

stand baptism as something by which evermore you die and live. . . . All our experience of life should be baptismal in character . . . to die and live by our faith in Christ.[2]

To lay hold of our baptismal promises together, Lutherans and Episcopalians—what a glorious day and what a glorious service! What care and planning it has taken, what years of prayer and labor lie behind it, what grace our Lord has shown to us in its coming to fruition. Symbolically, what could be more fitting than the location of this service within Lent? Today, with the Feast of the Incarnation nine months hence, the blessed Virgin Mary receives the implanted Word. She must live by promise; she must wait a long time; the purpose of God is only partially revealed; the way is dark; the consummation is not yet. It is an image of the church; but just as Mary sang "He has put down the mighty from their seats and has exalted the humble and meek" as if it had already happened, so we also sing by faith, "Christ is made the sure foundation, Christ the head and cornerstone . . . binding all the Church in one."[3] I must say that the proximity of Anglicanism's own Henry Purcell to the Lutheran titan Johann Sebastian Bach during this service reminds me of Flannery O'Connor's comparison of herself to William Faulkner as a donkey cart trying to get out of the way of the Dixie Limited roaring down the track. But surely someone made a most generous and happy decision to let us have Purcell's *Westminster Abbey* this afternoon instead of Luther's *Ein feste Burg*.

This is a moment of gratitude and awe for me as I think of my professor of homiletics, the great Lutheran preacher Edmund Steimle, rejoicing with us today in the communion of saints. May God bless the words of my mouth and the meditations of all our hearts.

"I Have Come to Do Thy Will"

The second lesson appointed for the Annunciation of the birth of our Lord Jesus Christ (Heb. 10:5–10) is a breathtaking example of the imaginative leaps characteristic of the Epistle to the Hebrews. God the Father and God

2. Martin Luther, "The Pagan Servitude of the Church," in *Martin Luther: Selections from His Writings*, ed. John Dillenberger (Garden City, NY: Anchor Books, 1961), on the principalities and powers, 294, 301–4.

3. This hymn is sung to the tune *Westminster Abbey*, by Anglican composer Henry Purcell.

the Son are seen working together from the beginning. The Son is speaking to the Father in words from the Old Testament—from Psalm 40. Christ speaks first (it seems) in his earthly form, then in his preincarnate form, then in his earthly form again. He seems to speak from *above*, face to face with the Father, saying, "Thou hast neither desired nor taken pleasure in sacrifices and offerings"; and he seems to speak from *below*, at the time when he comes into the world: "A body thou hast prepared for me." It's a brilliant passage and a brilliant choice for this Feast, as the Son offers himself up from before his earthly conception to be the perfect offering for our sanctification. Thus Christ speaks to the Father: "Lo, I have come to do thy will, O God," and the apostolic writer continues, "By that will we have been sanctified through the offering of the body of Jesus Christ once for all."

By that will. Let us ponder this. Our sanctification is accomplished by the will of God. Yet we live in a culture, today in America, in which we are famously certain that we are *self*-determined, *self*-created, *self*-invented. We routinely speak of reinventing our*selves*. We speak of *self*-care, *self*-motivation, *self*-chosen values without stopping to think about it. Indeed, it could be argued that self-determination is the great American gospel. All of us Lutherans and Episcopalians are affected by this. It is in the air we breathe and the water we drink. It has deeply affected the theology of every denomination. Yet it is not biblical. Jesus is our prototype: "Not my will, but thine, be done." "By that will we have been sanctified."

When I was sixteen years old, I saw a movie about Martin Luther (this was in the early fifties). It made an impression on me that has lasted my entire life.[4] That movie would probably seem very dated to us now, but its depiction of Luther perusing the Scriptures and finding there the revelation of God's justification of sinful humanity by grace through faith was in some ways the most crucial event in my life. I have loved blessed Martin ever since and have rejoiced to read his writings over the years. When I went back to them in preparation for this sermon, however, I was very surprised to discover that much of his work sounds different now that the cultural context has changed. All the great qualities are still there: the vitality and exuberance, the bold defense of the faith, the robust Protestant conscience, the single-minded passion for the person of Christ. But we do not live in a time like Luther's. Polemic is out of fashion. Episcopal ecumenical officer

---

4. This film, entitled simply *Martin Luther*, is available in a fiftieth anniversary edition on DVD. It is indeed dated; I cannot now recover the powerful impression that it made on me at the time, but its effects are with me still.

Philip Whitehead of Columbia, a leading figure in planning today's service, is quoted in yesterday's paper: "We've come back to the center, to Jesus Christ. We're really tired of the intricate differences that cause people to argue." That gracious statement captures the mood of today's America. Luther's vehemence, his sarcasm, his bite, and what one might call his "exclusiveness" do not sit well with the needs of today's church as we seek to come to terms with multiculturalism. But every theologian must be re-interpreted in each new generation. Let us see what a new reading of Luther might have to say to our present situation. I shall be following the lead of the great Lutheran New Testament theologian Ernst Käsemann, whose rereading of justification—especially in Romans—is the most radical.

Inclusion and Exclusion Arises Sharply in the New Testament

The watchword of the mainline churches today is "inclusivity." I venture to say that no other culture has ever made such a strenuous attempt to treat all kinds of people fairly and their religious beliefs respectfully as we are doing in America today. The point of mentioning this is that the move toward inclusion has arisen out of Christianity itself. Biblical prophecy, the teachings of our Lord and the example of countless Christians who have exemplified forbearance, charity, forgiveness, and solidarity with the op-pressed have pushed us further toward inclusiveness than any other society has ever gone. This is not to deny the church's lamentable guilt with regard to such horrors as the Crusades, the Inquisition, and Christian anti-Sem-itism. There is need for continual vigilance, but at the same time there is good reason to argue that the Judeo-Christian tradition has been (at the very least) a hospitable environment and (at the most) a driving force for human freedom.[5] Pressed to its logical conclusion, Christian faith does point toward radical inclusion. But this leads to a question. *What is the basis* for this unprecedented approach to human arrangements?

The question of inclusion and exclusion arises sharply in the New Tes-tament. The most obvious example is Jesus's table fellowship with sinners and tax collectors. In honor of Martin Luther, however, let us go directly

---

5. I have in mind the Enlightenment, land reform, universal literacy and health care, the abolitionist movement, the human rights movement, the civil rights movement, the women's movement, freedom of speech, freedom of religion, democracy, and perhaps most interestingly, secularization itself.

to the Epistle to the Galatians, where we find the two greatest figures in the New Testament church, Peter and Paul, at a church dinner having a public fight about inclusion and exclusion. We all know and love Peter for his all-too-obvious flawed humanity; true to character, he has gotten up from the non-kosher table and moved over to the kosher one. Why has he done that? For the same reason that, when I go to the Episcopal General Convention, I don't want to be seen hanging around the booths of the ultra-conservatives. For the same reason that George W. Bush doesn't want to be seen with Yasir Arafat right now. For the same reason that you might take your unattractive friend to lunch at an unfashionable restaurant where the in-crowd won't see you. Peter doesn't want the hotshots from Jerusalem to catch him eating with the unrighteous, so he scoots over to the other end of the room where the tables are filled with the politically correct. Paul recounts the story: "I opposed [Peter] to his face [that's Paul, for sure], because he stood condemned." Condemned for what? Condemned for being exclusionary, of course. But on what basis? Paul goes on: "We ourselves, who are [moral aristocrats] by birth and not [benighted] Gentile sinners, yet . . . *even we* have believed in Christ Jesus, in order to be justified by faith in Christ, and not by works of the law, because by works of the law shall no one be justified" (Gal. 2:11, 15–17). Those are not the reasons for inclusion usually given in the mainline churches today, at least not in my hearing. The reason usually given is "Jesus loves everybody." But is that a sufficient account of what Jesus does?

A remarkable column appeared just yesterday in the South Carolina *State* newspaper. It concerns the controversy about a proposed statue to honor Denmark Vesey, the free black man who was hanged in Charleston in 1822 along with thirty-five others when it was discovered that he was about to lead a massive slave rebellion which may or may not have resulted in the massacre of the white women and children of Charleston.[6] The column also refers to the recent appearance in Charleston of black writer Jamaica Kincaid, who spoke unkindly of John C. Calhoun at a garden club event in Charleston.[7] There were some who said that she had "unforgivably" offended against local hospitality. (This charge was also brought against Jesus as he dined in the homes of Pharisees.) The columnist describes the various viewpoints being expressed in South Carolina as "parallel universes," which

6. Claudia Smith Brinson, "State's Past on Collision with Future," *The State*, March 24, 2001.

7. This is recounted by Kincaid in *The New Yorker*, January 22, 2001.

exist without touching one another. To large numbers of white Southerners, John C. Calhoun is worthy of a statue and Denmark Vesey is not. To African Americans, Denmark Vesey is a freedom fighter and Calhoun is an oppressor. Can we communicate at all about this? asks the columnist. Is there any common ground? Is Jesus's love for each of these people enough to smooth over these drastic differences?

The rector of a large Episcopal parish recently told me the story of what happened when, in obedience to Jesus's teaching that we should pray for our enemies, he put Saddam Hussein on the prayer list at a Sunday service at the onset of the Gulf War. Three people stormed out of the church, the senior warden was apoplectic, and the congregation was in an uproar. The rector said it was the most genuinely frightening time of his life. The only thing that saved us, he said, was the brevity of the Gulf War.

Does Jesus love Saddam Hussein? Does he love fundamentalists? (I hope so, since I've been called one.) Does he love racists and homophobes and child molesters? Some of you may remember the vision of fellow Southerner Will Campbell, probably the only person in America who could get away with this: musing about unconditional grace, he imagines "Golda Meir chasing Hitler around the pinnacles of heaven, and after a thousand years he stops and lets her pin a Star of David on his chest."[8]

Is that enough? Can we really say that God loves Hitler? Don't we have to say something more than that? What does God's sanctification of the human race mean and how is it to be accomplished?

Our mutual friend Ernst Käsemann has helped us to see that the much-debated connection between justification and sanctification is in the biblical phrase that rings through Romans: *the righteousness of God.* Käsemann's reading of Romans led him to realize that justification is not simply a declaration of acquittal. Justification also means that God is actively and powerfully at work *making right what is wrong.*[9] Forgiveness in and of itself does not encompass the entire will of God. In order to grasp what God's future means for the world, we need to see that the action of God in Jesus Christ means not only the forgiveness of sins but also the rectification of all wrong. It is this insight that enables Paul to say, in Romans 8, "In all things God is working together for good." It enables him to say "I consider

8. Will D. Campbell, *And Also with You: Duncan Gray and the American Dilemma* (Franklin, TN: Providence House, 1997).

9. This is developed in the new Anchor Bible commentary on Galatians by one of Käsemann's postdoctoral students, J. Louis Martyn.

that the sufferings of this present time are not worth comparing with the glory that is to be revealed to us." When Paul says that "the whole creation waits with eager longing . . . to obtain the glorious liberty of the children of God," he means that the righteousness of God *is being* made and *will be* made real in human beings and in human society, not because we will it so, but because God wills it so. Jesus *does* love everybody, but that is not a sufficient theological basis to motivate us to include the Saddam Husseins and the child molesters of the world. We must say more. We must speak of the power of God working through the cross, resurrection, and second coming of his Son Jesus Christ to make all people righteous and all things right as they are meant to be.

The Freedom We Have in Christ Jesus

It may be that some of you are feeling lost in all this theological talk. What does all this mean for you personally? What does it mean for your *self*? And what does it mean for church life today?

It means freedom. It means what Paul calls in Galatians "the freedom we have in Christ Jesus" (Gal. 2:4 NRSV). It means joy in who you are and what you are without worrying so much about how you're doing. It means confidence; if you know that *God* is at work making right what is wrong, you can step along with what he is already doing without spending so much time being frustrated with other people. There was an amazing anecdote in the *New York Times* last year about the march from Charleston to Columbia to protest the display of the Confederate battle flag at the capitol across the street here. As the marchers were assembling at the starting point, a white man identified as Carter Sabo of Charleston stood alone on the sidelines holding the battle flag. "He stood briefly by Sandra and Tommie Gordon, an African-American couple from Maldin, and [as the marchers started out for Columbia] Ms. Gordon gave Mr. Sabo a hug."[10]

Where does that kind of redemptive action come from? It comes from the certainty that the righteousness of God is not going to leave us as we are, but is actively working for us and in us by the power of the Spirit, not only to forgive us, but to *rectify* us—to bring justification and sanctification together in us for our great good and for his great glory. *God's* work, dear

---

10. "Protest March Against Flag Attracts 600 in South Carolina," *New York Times*, April 3, 2000.

brothers and sisters, not ours. As Robert Farrar Capon has written, God did not come to love the loveable and improve the improveable, but to raise the dead.[11] And so let us come with joyful hearts to the table of the Lord who in his own body made the sacrifice for us all. Let us close as we began with the words of Martin Luther, who knew as well as any man that he needed some fixing up:

> When a person has lost Christ, he must fall into the confidence of his own works.[12]

> Take great care that no one goes to mass trusting in confession, or prayer, or self-preparation; but lacking confidence in all these things let him rather go in high confidence in the Christ who gives the promise.[13]

To the same Jesus Christ our Lord, and to the Father, and to the Holy Spirit be all might, majesty, dominion, and glory, now and for ever. Amen.

---

11. Robert Farrar Capon, *The Foolishness of Preaching* (Grand Rapids: Eerdmans, 2000).

12. Martin Luther, *Commentary on Galatians*, in Dillenberger, ed., *Martin Luther: Selections from His Writings*, 106.

13. Luther, "The Pagan Servitude of the Church," 281.

Old Adam, New Adam; Old World, New World; Old You, New You: Romans 5:12–21

William H. Willimon

Lent 1: For while we were still weak, at the right time Christ died for the ungodly. . . . But God proves his love for us in that while we still were sinners Christ died for us. . . . Yet death exercised dominion from Adam to Moses, even over those whose sins were not like the transgression of Adam, who is a type of the one who was to come. But the free gift is not like the trespass. For if the many died through the one man's trespass, much more surely have the grace of God and the free gift in the grace of the one man, Jesus Christ, abounded for the many. . . . If, because of the one man's trespass, death exercised dominion through that one, much more surely will those who receive the abundance of grace and the free gift of righteousness exercise dominion in life through the one man, Jesus Christ. Therefore just as one man's trespass led to condemnation for all, so one man's act of righteousness leads to justification and life for all. (Rom. 5:6, 8, 14–18 NRSV)

I tell my seminarians, when you get out of Duke Divinity and into your first pastorate, get close to alcoholics in your congregation. Work with them, have them promise to try harder to do better, make them sign pledges that they will stop drinking, stay up late with them and pray. That will do more to cure you of your little liberal, Sunday school, superficial theology than anything I know.

It's a terminal illness. They don't get better by sincerely wanting to get better.

As far as I know, I'm not an alcoholic, but I do have a history of dieting. "We've learned one thing about diets," a distinguished Duke physician recently said. "Diets don't work."

I stand on the bathroom scales, read the numbers, and cry, "Fake news!"

Dip your hand into that potato chip bag and promise the Lord that you will eat just one handful. Five minutes later your head is buried in the bag!

This human, all-too-human, inclination, this trappedness, Paul color-
fully calls "the old Adam." Remember old Adam? God put the first human-
oids in a lush garden, so rich and bountiful they didn't need to work. God
said, "Be fruitful and multiply" (the most gracious command God ever gave
us). Oh, and one other thing: "Stay off that tree over there." You can eat fruit
from the hundreds of other trees, but not that tree.

Well, you know the story. The minute God's back was turned, Adam
saw that the forbidden fruit looked tasty, even more appealing because of
God's prohibition.

"Did God say?" asked the serpent, the first theologian. "You won't die!"
So Adam took and ate, and Eve did the same, and let's just say human in-
nocence (if that's what it was) lasted for what, fifteen minutes?

It's been downhill ever since. Old Adam progressed, or regressed, from
that primal act of rebellion to misbehavior on a more cosmic scale. The
forbidden fruit is eaten, one of Adam's sons bashes in the head of the other,
strife between men and women who were created to be mutually fruitful,
raping and pillaging, wars and rumors of wars, terrorists and terror against
terrorists, liars and adulterers (for whom we voted). Our sin has gotten
loose into the whole cosmos, says Paul.

The Old Adam

Paul, in writing to First Church Rome, uses shorthand for all that rebellion—*the old Adam.*

Pick up the newspaper, read of some fresh deceit out of Washington,
the latest move of the powerful against the powerless—Paul wants you to
think, *Adam.* Try, really try to break some self-destructive habit and fail.
Paul says, "It's Adam all over again."

A physician sweeps his hand across the horizon of the Duke Medical
Center and says, "We figure that over half of those rooms are occupied by
patients who are sick because of bad lifestyle choices. Say, preacher, why
do we choose an early death over a longer life?"

"Well, you see," I explain, "it goes way back, even before the invention of
cigarettes, whiskey, and potato chips, back to our forebear, Adam, whose
DNA we've never been able to flush out of our systems."

When I hear of Trump's latest lie or racist gaff, I say, "I'd like to take one
of those cheap, tough Trump steaks and cram it down his lying little . . ."
Then Saint Paul says *to me,* "Sounds like your great, great granddaddy old

Adam. You are members of the same family. Only difference between you and The Donald is the color of your hair."

As we began a new millennium, President Bush proclaimed a "New World Order." How has that worked out? I voted for President Obama under the banner, "Yes we can!" No, we can't.

It's like I'm caught. As Paul said elsewhere, "I'm miserable! The good that I would do, I can't. Who will deliver me from this slavery to sin and death?" (Rom. 7:23–24). Sin is original (from our origins), universal (all), indomitable (can't think your way out of it), and undeniable. Old Adam.

An even more depressing aspect of being branches on Adam's family tree is that even our best attempts to do good are tainted by our bad. Nobody has ever started a war in order to do bad. We only kill by lethal injection or a drone in order to stop killing. I've never told a lie—except for somebody else's good. Old Adam.

When I was a sixteen-year-old at a church youth conference, the adults asked, "Since you are such a good Christian boy, would you be willing to have a black roommate here at the conference?" And I, nice Christian boy, said, "Sure, I'd love to self-validate my goodness."

We were from the same hometown, even though we went to different schools, different churches next door to each other. That Saturday, in a late-night conversation, he asked, "Does it bother you that you get on a Greenville city bus with a big sign, 'S.C. Law. Colored patrons sit from the rear. White patrons sit from the front'?"

"Uh, never thought about it, I guess," I replied.

"Does it bother you that neither you nor your church has ever thought about that sign?" The address of the old Adam? It's my America, my soul.

The United Methodist bishops, in a grand display of self-importance, voted to end malaria. The Episcopal bishops said, "We're not going to take that sitting down," and voted to end poverty. That led to the Methodist bishops promising to "end killer diseases in Africa." That's showing 'em!

As Paul put it, it's not only that I'm born and bred to lean toward the wrong; it's that I'm never more wrong than when I sincerely, earnestly try to put myself right. Old Adam is me all over.

Alcoholics Anonymous knows this, that huge first step of the twelve: "We admitted we were powerless over alcohol—that our lives had become unmanageable." Oh unmanageable me. Old Adam.

If we weren't all the offspring of old Adam, we wouldn't have had to begin this service with a Prayer of Corporate Confession, admitting that though we would like to make church the location for some minor moral tuning, a place where the good go to become a bit better, where we unleash our "better angels," church begins with the Adamic Confession, "We have erred and strayed from thy ways like lost sheep, we have followed too much the devices and desires of our own hearts, there is no health in us."

"I believe in man!" proclaimed William Faulkner when he got the Nobel Prize. He who wrote some of the most honest novels about the fallenness of the human condition flinched at the end, saying, "I believe in man"?

Oh, that's right, Faulkner was drunk when he said it.

I noted as a bishop that whenever there's a serious moral lapse among clergy, there's always someone to say, "Well, goes to show, pastors are only human."

Interesting. We use that phrase, "only human," to indicate us at our worst.

So old Adam is a nice metaphor, not just for the bad things we do, but also for who we are, down deep, from our first. Oh, we fantasize that we could just run the video in reverse, to a rerun of Eden, regurgitate the forbidden fruit, and get the old Adam out of our hardwiring.

Paul, in Romans, links sin with death. We're like some robot that attempts to go on its own by unplugging itself from the source of its life. It continues to run for a while, but the robot eventually goes dead. I've spent my ministry standing with many sad people who tried to live their lives on their own, who thought they had within themselves the key to the good life. It's a way that leads to death, sometimes death while you're still breathing.

"Who will rescue me from this body of death?" asks Paul. Our situation is such that we don't need some new technique, a fresh self-help program, or governmentally subsidized plan. Paul's right: we need nothing less than divine rescue.

That's one reason why I have loved the recovering alcoholics in my congregations and have regarded them as the closest thing we have to real saints. They have learned the truth about our infection by the old Adam the hard way and have dared to tell the truth about us.

A preacher in Houston (I'm not going to mention the name since I'm such a nice Christian boy) ladles out sweet bromides: "You are good. You mean well. These negative people keep trying to pull you down. Don't let 'em. You begin your day looking into the mirror and (repeat after me), 'I will have a good day.' 'I will do my best and be the best.'"

And I'm watching this and thinking, "They're Texans, for God's sake!"

No, I'm thinking, "Paul will never be allowed to preach from that pulpit."

Repentance is not when I say, "I will accept Jesus as my Savior. I will dedicate my life to Christ." Repentance begins in Lent when the church teaches me honestly to admit to the bad news about myself and the good news about God: "I can't choose God; I need a God who, wonder of wonders, chooses me." "If I'm going to be free to choose life rather than death, God will have to do it for me."

You can't make yourself right simply by resolving to do so. Sin isn't just your bad habits and unfortunate decisions. It's so deep in our thinking and acting that when we try to take matters in hand and solve our God problem, we produce more sin.

"Man produces evil like a bee produces honey," said the novelist William Golding.

Paul's Gospel in a Nutshell

Here's Paul's gospel in a nutshell: *In Christ, God has decisively, once and for all, done something about our sinful, death-dealing servitude.* Christ gets us out of the mess that the old Adam got us into. Whereas in Adam God was disobeyed, the new Adam, when presented (in this Sunday's Gospel) with the tempting offers of miraculous power, political clout, and freedom from suffering, said "No!" and Satan slinked away, defeated.

That's the good news Paul presents after his sober, pessimistic, yet truthful bad news. Adam is who we really are.

But who is God? God is Jesus Christ, whom Paul names the new Adam. Christ is the fresh start that we fantasized about but could never make for ourselves. The God whom we disobeyed and even crucified is determined to be God for us.

To put all this in context, the man who wrote this letter to First Church Rome in which he so soberly described the dead end that is the fate of the progeny of the old Adam, that man was the capo of the death squad that worked terrorist acts throughout Judea, Paul. He preached that the one whom we nailed to a cross responded by turning the other cheek, looked down on us, saying, "Father, forgive, they don't know, have never known, will not know what they are doing. Forgive 'em. It'll teach 'em a lesson."

Church, this is good news indeed—not that we have succeeded in loving God, but that in Christ God loves us. We were made by God, not to disobey and rebel, but to know and to live into this good news.

I can't explain it, but I can sing it: in the death and resurrection of Christ, God has made a fresh start with us, the world has been re-created, re-booted. We're not living in the realm of the old Adam with its dog-eat-dog-survival-of-the-fittest-we're-number-one-get-them-before-they-get-you deadness. We're in a whole new world where new Adam reigns.

I asked her why she liked being a Methodist. She responded, "I spent thirty-five years thinking God was mad at me. Then somebody told me the news that God loves sinners."

The new Adam (Christ) has brought us along with him through death and resurrection. It's a whole new ball game between us and God, as if God has gone back and restarted creation. When I was in the sixth grade, our teacher brought a scared little towheaded boy into our class and introduced him as a "misplaced person."

"He's come from Poland because he lost his family in the war. He's come here for freedom and a new life."

Jimmy Preston leaned over to me and said, "Poland must suck if displaced persons got to come to Greenville for a better life."

Well, we tried to help him with his English and get to know him. One problem, though. He stole our lunches. He stole food out of our lunch boxes. The teacher told him not to. He said he wouldn't. But almost every day somebody was in tears and the teacher uncovered the lost sandwich in his desk.

Janie Jones came crying to the teacher about her lost Twinkie. In desperation the teacher took hold of the displaced person and said, "Look at me! There's plenty of food now. You will never be hungry again. If you ever need food, ask me. You're in America. It's a whole new world."

And I tell you, looking into his eyes, I knew he understood. His eyes opened. He was in a whole new world. He never stole again.

Well, something like that has happened to us, says Paul. Wake up. We've been placed in a relationship with God that we couldn't make for ourselves. Elsewhere Paul proclaims, "If someone is in Christ, he is a new creation. The old has departed. Behold, he has become quite new" (2 Cor. 5:17).

That's you. What happens in baptism? They asked Martin Luther. Luther explained: in baptism the old Adam is drowned so that the new you can be born.

Christ has reinvented you, has reconstructed the world so that now God looks at you and smiles, "Yes! This is what I had in mind when I made you! Yes! Now, my new creation, go claim the new world."

Participationist Perspective

Death Becomes Her: Romans 6:1–14

Timothy G. Gombis

Death Becomes Her is the title of a comedy from the early 1990s starring Meryl Streep and Goldie Hawn. If you haven't seen it, you are missing nothing, but the title lingered in my mind as I pondered this text in Romans and the situation we face. We are in a season of discernment over where our community is headed. We have experienced great blessing over the past few years as we have ministered in the midst of this neighborhood, and we have all grown in significant ways. But where do we go from here?

This is the question with which the Shepherd Team has sat over the last few months, and our discussions have been vigorous. Word about those conversations has spread among the rest of us, and we are wondering what exactly comes next. For my part, I am confident that I know the way forward, and I believe I have reasons for such confidence. After all, reflection on New Testament biblical-theological conceptions of the people of God and how the church participates in the mission of God is my full-time job. I am a member of the guild of New Testament scholars, and so I have pondered at great length how all of this relates to our little community and its mission. As I talk with others that I know agree with me, I have grown even more certain that my conception of things is the life-giving path. I have found our many discussions over direction to be mostly fruitful, but I

Preaching is, at the very least, a word on target for a particular community facing specific challenges and opportunities. Paul's Letter to the Romans is a gospel word on target to help a community being threatened by division. I was part of the Shepherd Team of a missional church called Midtown Christian Community when we experienced a season of tension over the direction our community would take. Paul's counsel based on the death/life paradox and participation in Christ helped me understand the dynamics unfolding in the relationships among our leadership and shaped my preaching during that time. Rather than addressing this sermon to no one in particular, I have directed it to the community I had the delight of inhabiting, and it represents what I would have said to them.

have grown frustrated at the resistance of a few people to see the brilliance of the vision I have laid out.

I hope you can discern that I am being facetious. Much of what I have to say is by way of confession. Over the past few weeks I have been reflecting on Pauline passages in which the apostle counsels churches in conflict, considering exhortations such as "If . . . you bite and devour one another, take care that you are not consumed by one another" (Gal. 5:15).[1] On one hand, I feel that I have been leading our community toward life and promise. Yet, on the other, I have begun to wonder whether I have been introducing dynamics of death as I have come to have great confidence in my own vision and have become convinced that others are resisting my wisdom out of sinister motives. In the counterintuitive, upside-down, and inside-out wisdom of God, resisting death and grasping after life has a paradoxical effect. It leads to frustration, discouragement, and division. Self-confidence can turn out to be self-deception. Viewing those who disagree as "opponents" of an obviously God-given ministry vision may end up being the path of self-destruction and community discouragement.

Experiencing the Life of God by Embracing Death

In the wisdom of God, the church experiences the life of God by embracing death. Many of us grew up singing "his banner over me is love," but the Pauline version might be "his banner over us is 'Death Becomes Her.'" As counterintuitive as it sounds, death is the promising identity marker for the church, since we all together experience the life-giving presence of Christ by his Spirit as we creatively inhabit his death. That entails the death of our ambition, the crucifixion of passion for our own vision and the plans and schemes we have for this community. Thanks be to God that our certificate of debt is nailed to the cross (Col. 2:14), but so must any proposed vision statement if it generates dynamics of discouragement, alienation, bitterness, and strife.

But here's the rub: this goes against how we are wired. Our self-preservation impulse is fierce, so we resist this. We do everything we can to avoid loss. We fear that we will not be heard in discussions over vision, and so the cross strikes us immediately as perilous. If I were honest, I'd admit that I want *others* to embrace the cross. I might even be interested in giving them

---

1. Scripture quotations are from the NRSV.

a hand to get on it! For myself, however, I would rather avoid it. But I have had to ask myself during this season whether I truly am owning my identity as one marked by the cross, or whether I am growing frustrated and a bit angry and perhaps have done damage with my attitudes and words. My imagination has been activated with all sorts of arguments that I am right. But now that I have stepped back to reflect, I've had to face the reality that I have seen the cross as good news for others and bad news for me. That's a perilous and deadly place to be—to see the cross of Christ as something to avoid.

But the cross is the most overpoweringly promising and overwhelmingly hopeful cosmic location, for anything and everything on the cross becomes a site upon which God pours out resurrection power. Our only hope of redemption and renewal as a community is to inhabit together the cross of Christ, holding very loosely our plans and ambitions for what is next. That participation will be embodied by community practices of listening, regarding each other with love, giving each other the benefit of the doubt, and being more committed to one another than to any particular vision.

The Roman Christians face a similar situation. Two groups have formed around divergent visions of how to embody faithful Christian discipleship to God. One group has a high regard for Scripture, and so they believe that loyalty to the God of Israel who sent Jesus as Savior means obeying the Scriptures of Israel by living as Jews. They maintain that they have Scripture and tradition on their side. They have summarized their position in a succinct, biblically driven slogan: "To the Jew first and then to the Greek." The other group is equally committed to Scripture, but they disagree about the first group's conclusions and are resisting the pressure to take on Jewish practices. The result of this split among the Roman Christians is discouragement. They are divided. And they are wondering if it is worth it to continue on as a community.

A Radically New Place Called "Grace"

Paul writes to encourage and unite them in their shared Christian identity. He instructs them that they are not to be passing judgment on one another, since they are all united together in their shared history of humanity under judgment (Rom. 1:18–3:20). And they have all been justified on the same basis, which makes them siblings in the family of Jesus, removing any basis on which any group can assert their claims against the other (3:21–31).

They live together in a radically new place called "grace" (5:2), redemptive cosmic space in which they have all been united to God and to one another. In fact, they inhabit God together by virtue of their being united to Christ by the power of the Spirit.

In Romans 6:1–14, Paul explains the paradoxical manner in which this new cosmic space is inhabited. Their participation in Christ—this new creation space—runs against the grain of how human imagination works. While each group is tempted to "fix" the other, advocating for their group's conception of Christian discipleship, their judging the other as wrong is actually serving the cosmic power of Sin! The way to faithfully inhabit the space of grace is not to go on sinning! And what Paul has in mind here is each group's tendency to pass judgment on the other. Paul's terms make it sound outrageous. Who would do this? Who would try to make the space of grace flourish and grow by sinning? But this is precisely what they're doing when they pass judgment on one another.

This is sobering. I know I've done this when I have become so convinced of the rightness of my own conception that I have dismissed others as being ill-informed or badly motivated. God's goal for our community is not a brilliant vision statement but mutual embrace, the offer of hospitality to one another and a unity marked by deep commitment to one another. What is nonnegotiable is that we stay together and look after each other, not that this or that side wins.

At our baptisms, we were plunged into Christ by the Spirit, and that means that the Spirit drove us deeply into the death of Christ. In this liberative realm—this new terrain of freedom we inhabit—we do not have the option of living under the reign of Sin by doing damage to one another, by coercing one another to see things our way. We have died to that realm, being delivered out of it through our participation in the death of Christ so that we now participate in the life of Christ. We have died to those patterns of community life that leave us empty-hearted and alienated, that destroy relationships and ruin friendships. We are tempted to hold tightly to what we want and to what is familiar, and we may feel that we are pointing the community toward blessing by doing so. But we're hurting each other and we're crushing community.

Only when we see the beauty of participating in the death of Christ through cultivating community patterns of peacemaking and mutual love and service; only when we see that the most promising place to be is on a cross will we have the hope of experiencing God's power among us. Indeed, "death becomes her"—death makes the church a beautiful place to be—in the sense that we experience the power of Christ's resurrection and we walk in the newness of life when we give ourselves over to death, as much as that runs counter to our sense of self-preservation and self-advancement.

And death is even more promising than that. Not only do we enjoy the life of God in Christ in our community *now* by ever more faithful participation in his death, but we guarantee that we will share in the joy of resurrection in the future when he comes to judge the living and the dead. "For if we have been united with him in a death like his, we will certainly be united with him in a resurrection like his" (6:5).

May God grant to each of us, in Christ and by the Spirit, the eyes to see the promise of the cross, and hearts of love for one another so that our community becomes a site on which God pours out resurrection life and power for the glory of God and the good of the world. Amen.

15

Made New by One Man's Obedience: Romans 5:12–19

Richard B. Hays

Listen to our text for today, from the fifth chapter of the apostle Paul's Letter to the Romans:

> Therefore, just as Sin came into the world through one man, and Death through Sin, and thus Death spread throughout the human race, with the result that all sinned—
>
> (For before the Law came, Sin was indeed in the world,
> but, since there was no Law, sin was not counted up;
> nonetheless, Death reigned. Death reigned from Adam to Moses,
> even over those who did not sin in the likeness of the transgres-
>   sion of Adam[by violating a commandment].)
>
> Now Adam is the prefiguration of the Coming One.
>
> But the grace-gift is *not* like the false step.
> For if by the false step of the one man the many died,
> *how much more* has the grace of God overflowed
> by means of the grace of the one man Jesus Christ to the many.
>
> And the gift is *not* like the effect of the one man's sin.
> For the judgment issuing from the sin of one led to condemnation;

Originally preached at York Chapel, Duke Divinity School, February 17, 2005 (revised and updated August 8, 2017). Texts: Gen. 2:15–17; 3:1–7; Matt. 4:1–11; Rom. 5:12–19. This chapter is a revised version of Richard B. Hays, "Made New by One Man's Obedience," from pages 96–102 of *Proclaiming the Scandal of the Cross*, edited by Mark D. Baker, published by Baker Academic, a division of Baker Publishing Group, copyright 2006. Used by permission.

but the grace-gift following upon many false steps leads to
vindication.
For if, by virtue of the one man's false step, Sin reigned through
the one man,
how much more will those who receive the superabundance of
grace and of the gift of
righteousness—how much more will they reign in life through
the one man Jesus Christ.

So then, as through the false step of one man condemnation
came to us all,
so also through the righteous act of one man the rectifying of life
came to us all.
For just as through the disobedience of one man the many were
constituted as sinners,
so also through the obedience of one man the many were constituted as righteous.

Romans 5:12–19 (my trans.)

If the apostle Paul had turned this passage in to me as a short theological reflection paper, I would have told him, "Get thee to the writing tutor." Then I would have called up the Writing Center and told them, "This guy Paul has some weighty ideas, but you really need to help him with this essay. First of all, he begins it with a sentence fragment. Then he goes off on a couple of digressions before he gets back to his main point. And he keeps repeating himself; it looks like he was trying out different formulations on the word processor, and then just turned in his rough draft without going back to edit it. The logical transitions are awkward. Finally, he could really use some illustrations to help us follow the point he's trying to make. I hope you can straighten him out so that he can pass my course on Greek Exegesis of Romans."

Joking aside, I suspect that the difficulty we have with this passage signals that it is we, not Paul, who need remedial work. At the superficial level, we need remedial work because we have lost the patience and skill necessary to follow intricately woven theological arguments. We would prefer our theology articulated in tweets or sound bites—or at least in *USA Today* prose aimed at a fifth-grade reading level. But the deeper truth is this: we need remedial work because we have followed our father Adam on the slippery path of false steps, and we have fallen. So now we find ourselves under the sway of the powers of Sin and Death. And living under these illusion-spinning powers, we have lost sight of the true story that makes sense of our lives.

Where then shall we begin the remediation? I would suggest a four-step program to let our minds be remade. Each step requires a fresh recognition of our human predicament and the unexpected way in which God has rescued us from ourselves.

Caught in the Web of Sin and Death

First, we have to recognize our true condition as people caught in the web of Sin and Death. We don't like to think about that. We like to believe that we've got things under control, that we are good down deep, and that all the world's problems come not from ourselves but from somewhere else— whether from undocumented immigrants and terrorists, or from some shadowy right-wing conspiracy. We like to believe that given enough time and ingenuity, we will solve our problems and "build a better world." Do we fear violence? We can solve that problem: we just have to kill all the bad people. (I saw a bumper sticker the other day, though, that said, "We're making enemies faster than we can kill them.") Social and economic ills? We just need to elect the right candidates and appoint the right Supreme Court justices. Psychological problems? We just need to find the right pre-scription drugs to achieve equilibrium. Our universities and corporations are engaged now in fierce competition to perfect techniques of genetic engineering so that we can redesign our own bodies and eliminate the flaws. O brave new world! Even death is sometimes regarded as a problem medical science has not yet solved . . . but give us time. Some of you may remember the gruesome fate of Ted Williams, the great Boston Red Sox slugger who died a number of years ago: after his death, his son had his body frozen to preserve it (hung upside down in a tank of liquid nitrogen at 325 degrees below zero) in the hope that a future medical science would find a way to restore life. (I guess if the Red Sox—and now even the Cubs— can win the World Series, anything is possible!) But here is my point: our naive trust in technology to cure all human ills actually bears witness to our pathetic, self-deceiving desire to hide from our own mortality, and our own sinfulness.

In the opening chapters of Romans, Paul hammers relentlessly on this theme. Like Adam and Eve, we have turned away from God into disobedience, and the end of our proud attempt to be "like God, knowing good and evil" is that we fall into idolatry, confusion, and self-destructive violence— all the while imagining ourselves to be virtuous. So the story of Adam holds a mirror before us, a mirror in which we can begin to glimpse our nakedness and shame. Adam's story is our story. And once that story is set in motion, human history becomes a chain reaction of deception, hiding behind fig leaves, and violence. The second chapter in the story of Adam is the story of Cain and Abel. If you want a clear image of what that chapter looks like, I urge you to see the film *Hotel Rwanda*, which tells a story of horrific ethnic violence in one small African country. It's a microcosm of the larger human condition. Or, if you want an image closer to home, just watch your television for heart-rending news of the latest school shooting.

The Overwhelming Good News

The second step in our remediation is not to be overwhelmed by the grimness of our own situation. Not because it isn't terrible, but because the gospel offers the overwhelming good news that "Christ died for the ungodly" (Rom. 5:6 NRSV). Despite our blindness and violence, we have now received reconciliation through Jesus Christ. One of the striking features of Romans 5:12–19 is Paul's adamant insistence on the *asymmetry* between sin and grace. Listen: "But the grace-gift is *not* like the false step. For if by the false step of the one man the many died, *how much more* has the grace of God overflowed by means of the grace of the one man Jesus Christ to the many." That "how much more" (*pollō mallon*) is the hallmark of Paul's gospel. As the New Testament scholar Paul Achtemeier puts it in his commentary on this passage, "Thus does grace triumph over evil, by burying evil in an avalanche of grace."[1]

That is why the analogy between Adam and Christ is *only* an analogy. Our solidarity with Adam in sin, confusion, and death is a pale, negative, two-dimensional shadow of our much more vivid, positive, three-dimensional solidarity with Jesus Christ. Curiously, our powers of perception are so impaired that we find it easier to grasp our solidarity with the old death-bound humanity in Adam than to grasp our participation in the new life-giving humanity into which Christ's death and resurrection have

---

1. Paul J. Achtemeier, *Romans*, Interpretation Commentary (Atlanta: John Knox, 1985), 102.

placed us. That is why Paul reminds us of Adam: to give us a clue, a mental handhold from which we can begin to grope toward imagining how our destiny can be determined by the action of a single great figure who comes before us and shapes the reality in which we live. But the Adam-Christ analogy should never mislead us into thinking that Jesus Christ merely undoes the effects of Adam's transgression and puts us back at square one with a blank slate; rather, Jesus has swept us into a new creation in which our identity is now positively redefined by *his* faithfulness rather than by our own disloyalty to God.

The Obedience of Jesus Christ

This way of speaking already points to a third step, a third crucial recognition. (And I select the word *crucial* carefully.) According to Romans 5, it is the *obedience* of Jesus Christ on which our salvation hangs. Recall how we got into our present predicament: Adam broke the commandment, and death entered the world. Israel violated the Sinai covenant, came under the curse, and went away into exile. But the story of Jesus's temptation in the wilderness reveals that something new has happened in the world. Jesus reveals himself as the new Adam who rejects the temptation to be like God and to seize power. Jesus also reveals himself as the true Israel who rightly honors the Torah by resisting the devil's temptation and taking refuge in the words of Deuteronomy 6: "Worship the Lord your God, and serve only him" (Matt 4:10 NRSV, citing Deut 6:13 LXX). And that wilderness temptation is a dress rehearsal for the true climax of Israel's story. The surprising climax is this: Jesus's obedience extends all the way to his death on a cross, still embodying his fervent prayer: "May your will be done." That is how Jesus's obedience quite literally initiates a new humanity, a new creation. Because of him and in him, the story can begin again.

Liberated to Participate in the Life of the World to Come

Finally, Romans 5 offers us a fourth step. As we seek to undertake the remedial work of allowing Paul's gospel to transform our minds, we must ask, "*In what way* does the obedient death of Jesus actually bring about our reconciliation with God?" (Or, to use the language of the systematic tradition, what theory of atonement do we find in Romans 5?)

In the Protestant tradition, particularly in its evangelical forms, we are used to interpreting the atonement chiefly in terms of blood sacrifice and penal substitution: Jesus paid the penalty that rightly was ours; Jesus shed his blood as a victim in order to cleanse us from guilt and sin—and perhaps to appease the wrath of God. (Note that the language of blood atonement will show up in our final hymn: Jesus's blood is a "crimson tide" that will wash away the "dark stain" of our sin.) To be sure, Paul does occasionally use images of substitutionary atonement (e.g., Rom 3:24–25; 5:9). Yet such references are surprisingly rare. Paul almost never talks about "forgiveness of sins," because—and here is the key point—he has a more radical diagnosis of the human predicament and a more radical vision of new creation. What we need is something far more than forgiveness or judicial acquittal. We don't just need to be forgiven; we need to be *changed*. We need to be set free from our bondage to decay and liberated to participate in the life of the world to come, a life that has already invaded our broken world. Strikingly, in Romans 5:12–19, nothing is said about blood sacrifice or about Jesus taking our punishment. The Adam-Christ typology offers a very different picture of the way in which we are saved: we are saved because we participate in the new humanity that Jesus, the faithful and obedient one, inaugurated.

How shall we picture this? Consider this analogy. Sometimes a computer can become so infected by a virus or malware that it is necessary to erase the memory on the hard disk and start over, reinstalling the software—including the operating system—and rebooting the machine. That is a distant analogy to what Paul is saying in Romans 5. It is as though the human race in Adam had become so infected by the virus of sin that malfunctions and "illegal operations" were paralyzing the system. Jesus, by virtue of his radical obedience to God, erases the infected program and installs a new virus-resistant operating system, enabling us to function rightly for the purpose for which we were made: he is Humanity 2.0.

Of course, we are not machines, and for that reason I worry about this analogy. Perhaps it is more like this: we are a dysfunctional family caught in cycles of bitterness, infidelity, conflict, addiction, and abuse. Jesus arrives in the midst of our domestic troubles—a mysterious, long-lost older brother—and transforms the family by living in a new self-giving way that astonishingly infuses a new spirit, changes the destructive dynamics, and refocuses the family on the love of God. His faithfulness not only *models* a different pattern of life but actually *creates* a new kind of family.

Once again, analogy falls short. I find myself wanting to say, like Paul, "But the grace-gift is not like the virus-riddled computer; how much more has the grace of God overflowed by means of the grace of the one man Jesus Christ." Or again, "But the grace-gift is not like the dysfunctional family; how much more has the grace of God overflowed by means of the grace of the one man Jesus Christ." This overflow of grace has actually *constituted* us as a new people, a new creation. God's love is poured into our hearts, and the Spirit is at work transforming us into the image of Jesus, the One who was faithful to the end, for our sake. That is the reality toward which all our analogies grope. And so we have peace with God, through our Lord Jesus Christ.

Thanks be to God.

16

Breathing Well: Romans 8:12–30

Suzanne Watts Henderson

We inhabit a world plagued by chronic breathing problems. Asthma, allergies, COPD, pulmonary fibrosis: diagnoses of a range of conditions that constrict our deep breathing have sky-rocketed in recent decades. Scientists pin the trend on a variety of environmental and genetic issues, but make no mistake, more of us have a harder time breathing than ever before.

But it's not just physical maladies that impair our ability to breathe well. On our own streets and across our globe, powerful systems conspire against the well-being of targeted groups, often through violent means. Since Eric Garner's 2014 death at the hands of law enforcement, the phrase "I can't breathe" has become a refrain for those crushed—suffocated, really—by oppression in myriad forms and settings.

Several years ago, the integrative medicine doctor Andrew Weil—made popular by Oprah and Dr. Oz—visited our campus. At an afternoon question and answer session, a student asked, "What's the one thing you would most recommend to improve our overall health?" Weil's answer was as reflexive as it was succinct: "As a society, we need to learn to breathe well."

Learning to Breathe Well

Our passage from Paul's Letter to the Romans is all about learning to breathe well. But it's a point that's easy to miss. After all, most English Bibles translate Paul's word *pneuma* as "spirit," or even "Spirit." That leads many Western Christians to jump to the doctrine of the Trinity and equate this *pneuma* with the third person of the Godhead.

But Paul's use of the word is hard to categorize and even harder to dogmatize. *Pneuma* appears twenty-one times in the chapter's thirty-nine verses, and it's not always clear whose "spirit" Paul is talking about: God's spirit? Christ's? Ours? Short answer: all of the above.

Like its Hebrew counterpart *ruach*, *pneuma* can also mean "wind" or "breath." This *pneuma* is a willy-nilly, whimsical force that imparts divine life wherever it shows up in the world. For Paul, this *pneuma* is divine breath that merges with our breath so that we might "have life, and have it abundantly" (John 10:10).[1] This *pneuma*, Paul wants us to grasp, is God's antidote for our breathing problems.

In some ways, this is not news, for Paul or any other readers of Scripture. After all, the Lord God has been breathing life into us from the beginning, ever since filling those first dusty nostrils with the "breath of life" (Gen. 2:7). Divine, life-giving breath shows up again as Ezekiel contemplates a valley filled with dry bones. Silly Ezekiel, he thought dead meant dead; he thought God's beleaguered, exiled people would go the way of human decay. But here comes the punchline: "Thus says the Lord GOD to these bones: I will cause breath to enter you, and you shall live" (Ezek. 37:5). It's not surprising, then, that the prophet Joel speaks this promise about the final restoration of the world: "I will pour out my breath upon all flesh" (Joel 2:28). From start to finish, the biblical story says that God's spirit, God's breath, fills lungs with new life, just when we need it most.

As Paul reads the tea leaves, the "day of the Lord" Joel anticipated has dawned in Christ's death and resurrection. This "Christ event," he thinks, has secured a foothold for God's life-giving power on earth. For Paul, the resuscitation of a good-as-dead Messiah offered an early indicator—the "first fruits," as he puts it (Rom. 8:23)—of God's breath at work to renew the whole cosmos. That divine, life-giving spirit, Paul thinks, is loose among the faithful in Rome. I'd suggest it might be loose among the faithful in our midst today.

A Compulsion to Be Led by God's Spirit

Let's be honest: those of us who identify as mainline Protestants can get a little twitchy when we start talking about the Holy Spirit. We've ceded that realm to the Pentecostals, thank you very much. We have intellect and reason going for us; we like dogma and systems, classifications and distinctions. For its part, the spirit is an unpredictable, haphazard force that resists our best efforts to domesticate it.

After centuries of hush-hush on the topic, though, even Western scholars are taking note of the divine *pneuma*. Philip Jenkins studies the church

---

1. All biblical quotations come from the NRSV, unless otherwise noted.

in the global south, where he detects in Pentecostalism the most "success-ful social movement of the past century"—not just numerically, but as a palpable witness to God's life-giving power.[2] For her part, the late Phyllis Tickle insisted that we stand on the cusp of what she calls "the age of the spirit." In her book by that title, she makes the case for the spirit's role in revitalizing the church today.[3]

Almost two thousand years ago, Paul made a similar case to a commu-nity devoted to a Jewish Messiah named Jesus. It was a timely message for the minority group, who lived as "resident aliens" under the kind of impe-rial system that caused a few breathing problems of its own. It's a timeless message for a world still gasping for a deep, cleansing breath. How might the divine *pneuma* constitute remedy for our breathing problems today?

Notice, first of all, the way this *pneuma* operates. It *leads* us (Rom. 8:14), for one thing. One interpreter puts it this way: when we're led by the spirit, we're "constrained by a compelling force, . . . surrendering to an overpow-ering compulsion."[4] In other words, God's spirit can have the same power over us as an addiction. Imagine being as overwhelmed by a compulsion to be led by God's spirit as we are to check our devices or eat potato chips or pour another glass.

By the same token, Paul says we *receive* this breath (Rom. 8:15) as some-thing of a gift. Compelling as this remedy for our breathing problems may be, it won't force itself on us. Only by exhaling all the way down, my yoga instructor might say, do we avail ourselves of the gift that's already ours: the mingling of our breath with the very breath of God. For Paul, the divine *pneuma* comes in alongside our *pneuma* (Rom. 8:16), much as a hospice caretaker comes in alongside the family of a dying patient.

Becoming Full-Fledged Members of the Divine Household

And the most amazing thing happens when this spirit mingles with ours: we become full-fledged members of the divine household. In the ancient world, "family values" assigned social and economic status based on one's

2. Philip Jenkins, *The Next Christendom: The Coming of Global Christianity*, 3rd ed. (New York: Oxford University Press, 2011), 10.

3. Phyllis Tickle with John M. Sweeney, *The Age of the Spirit: How the Ghost of an An-cient Controversy Is Shaping the Church* (Grand Rapids: Baker Books, 2014).

4. James D. G. Dunn, *Romans 1–8*, Word Biblical Commentary 38 (Dallas: Word Books, 1988), 450.

place in the household. Paul turns those family values on end in several ways. For one thing, his language vacillates between the gendered word "son" and the gender-neutral word "child." Such a move dismantles stratified distinction between male and female, even defying conventional practice by naming as God's "heirs" not "sons" but "children" (Rom. 8:17). As a result, the status of "sonship" is "broadened beyond ethnic, familial, imperial, legalistic, and educational barriers" in addition to gendered ones.[5]

But Paul doesn't stop there. In a statement that might give us pause, he says this change-of-status that happens when we breathe the divine *pneuma* even elides the distinction between us and Christ: we are "heirs of God and joint heirs with Christ" (Rom. 8:17). As Christ is God's "son," so are we. God's estate, so to speak, will be split evenly among us.

And yet. As if Paul knows how alluring this whole inheritance business might be—how easily it morphs into a prosperity gospel or a theology of glory—he returns us straightaway to the "sufferings of the present time" (Rom. 8:18). Paul's no fool. He knows that those who breathe God's breath will inevitably find themselves in the crosshairs of conflict, where death-dealing systems still hold creation hostage, in "bondage to decay" (Rom. 8:21). Jesus certainly did, the Roman Christians did, and so too do we.

It's into the midst of these "labor pains" (Rom. 8:22) that the deep breath of God supplants our shallow, fearful panting with oxygenated hope. Let's be clear: God's spirit comes not as an epidural that anesthetizes us but as a life-giving power through which pain brings new life. This is how Paul dares to say that "all things work toward the good for those who love God, for those called to be on public display" for the power of life in the midst of death (Rom. 8:28, my trans.).

If we have eyes to see, we can catch glimpses of such "public display," snapshots of those whose breath mingles with God's breath in ways that sparkle with life and hope amid stultifying and suffocating conditions. I think of Nadine Collier, whose mother was one of the Emanuel Nine who died at a Charleston Bible study in 2015. Given the chance to address Dylann Roof at his bond hearing just days after the shooting, Ms. Collier began with the words, "I forgive you." A year later, I heard her explain it this way: "People criticized me for these words, but honestly, as a Christian, did I really have any choice? I'd spent my whole life learning Jesus's way of forgiveness. It's the only way not to suffocate from hatred."

---

5. Robert Jewett, *Romans: A Commentary*, Hermeneia (Minneapolis: Fortress, 2007), 497.

I think too of Daoud Nasser and his family, whose Tent of Nations farm outside Bethlehem creatively resists the Israeli government's attempt to choke them off. Their "public display" can be seen painted on a stone on their property: "We refuse to be enemies." Denied access to water, they collect rain in cisterns; denied building permits, they create guest houses in caves; cut off from the electrical grid, they capture the power of the sun. Mostly, they continue to breathe the very breath of God, the breath of life and love that's stronger than death-dealing force.

How are your breathing patterns these days? Do you find yourself suffering from shortness of breath? Suffocating under oppressive systems or relationships or conditions that suck the life out of you? Or standing in solidarity with those who are?

Paul has some good news for you and for me. God's spirit is loose in the world; God's breath can yet fill our lungs with new life. May we, as individuals and as God's people, learn again to breathe well. Filled with and led by God's very breath, may we show the world what God's life-giving power looks like even—or perhaps especially—as death lets out its last-ditch efforts to destroy. Animated by God's breath, may we live in our sure hope that death has indeed lost its sting (1 Cor. 15:55). Thanks be to God.

CONCLUSION

17

Implications

Joseph B. Modica

One may conclude after reading the essays and sermons in this volume that one should choose the "right" perspective on the apostle Paul. Or perhaps that one perspective unties all the interpretive knots. Or even that one perspective is more true (i.e., "more Christian") or more accurate than the others. That, however, is not the intended purpose of this volume. This does not mean that those who argue for or preach from a certain perspective are not convinced of its interpretive lens. Rather, one should view these perspectives as an interpretive kaleidoscope, so to speak. Thus one can appreciate and evaluate the contributions of these perspectives, which can deeply enrich one's understanding of the apostle Paul and his letters.

Why do these different perspectives exist? Why are they even important? It seems that the perspectives exist because interpreters exist. Like the quest for the historical Jesus, the perspectives on the apostle Paul serve similar ends. The raison d'etre is to understand the apostle Paul and his letters. Perhaps the best way to evaluate these perspectives is to view them as contributions—and not threats—to the vast terrain of interpretations. Different perspectives can yield beneficial outcomes.

The perspectives represented in this volume are not the only ones available. One recent addition is the "Paul within Judaism" perspective, sometimes referred to as the "radical new perspective." Here interpreters argue that Paul critiques the law *only* for gentiles, not Jews. Hence, Jews are still to be torah observant as followers of Jesus, which would include the apostle himself.[1] This volume includes the perspectives that, according to the co-

---

1. See one noted proponent, Mark D. Nanos, especially "A Jewish View," in *Four Views on the Apostle Paul*, ed. Michael F. Bird (Grand Rapids: Zondervan, 2012), 159–93, and

---

Many thanks to Scot McKnight, longtime friend and coeditor, for his helpful comments on an earlier version of this essay.

editors, cohere with an understanding of the apostle Paul as a transformed or reoriented (see Acts 9) follower of Jesus the risen Messiah. He doesn't necessarily leave his Judaism behind, but he now has a different telos—to preach that Jesus Christ is the fulfillment of Israel's story.[2]

Observations

So we have the Reformational, new, apocalyptic, and participationist perspectives on the apostle Paul. I would like to make four general observations.

1. Each perspective is an earnest attempt to interpret the Letter to the Romans.

No one perspective on the apostle Paul solves all the interpretive dilemmas. Some may effectively argue that a certain perspective does much better than another, but it would be foolhardy to rely solely on one perspective or to argue that one's perspective is the only true one. Interpretive convictions are not the same as certainties. Appreciating the various perspectives on the apostle Paul makes one a more effective and gracious interpreter.

So what then do these perspectives contribute to a kaleidoscope understanding of the apostle Paul? Here's a very brief highlight of each.

First, the *Reformational perspective* offers as its central emphasis the sacrificial death of Jesus for humans, who are all under God's judgment. All human beings are sinful and in need of God' redemption. Hence, God has provided redemption through the righteous death of Jesus. Since no one's merits can earn one's salvation, God finds righteous those who place their faith in Jesus Christ. Stephen Westerholm aptly observes: "Like soup and sandwich, faith and grace go together; 'works' and grace do not."[3] Subsequently, for the apostle Paul, Jesus's death fundamentally changed the relationship between Jews and gentiles.

The *new perspective's* capstone is its new way of understanding Judaism. E. P. Sanders's magnum opus, *Paul and Palestinian Judaism*, which,

---

"Paul and Judaism: Why Not Paul's Judaism?," in *Paul Unbound: Other Perspectives on the Apostle*, ed. Mark D. Given (Peabody, MA: Hendrickson, 2010), 117–60.

2. Thus, the "Paul within Judaism" perspective does not fit the Christocentric telos lens of understanding the apostle Paul and his relationship to his churches.

3. See p. 18.

as others have noted, is more about a new perspective of Judaism than a new perspective on Paul. Scot McKnight asks an important question: "Is Sanders a *participant in* or the *preparation for* the new perspective?"[4] The most important element of the new perspective, according to McKnight, is "its reaction to previous voices [i.e., Christian scholarship] and its renewed interest in an organic understanding of Judaism itself."[5] One continues to see the various iterations of the new perspective among its main proponents (e.g., Wright, Dunn). Perhaps Sanders did cultivate a fertile field from which the new perspective blossomed. One could then argue that the new, the apocalyptic, and the participationist perspectives are attempts to come to terms with Paul following Sanders.

The *apocalyptic perspective*, anchored in the seminal work of J. Louis Martyn in North America, sees the apostle Paul's gospel message as a reaction to theological foundationalism and focuses on the epistemology of Paul's revelation (note the title of Martyn's influential 1967 essay, "Epistemology at the Turn of the Ages").[6] What does Jesus reveal? Jesus is the revelatory truth from God to humanity. Paul's gospel, then, is situated in an "apocalyptic construal," says Douglas Campbell.[7] Hence, Campbell notes that one must tell this apocalyptic story backward or retrospectively to fully understand the apostle Paul's perspective. There is an inherent danger, Campbell wisely notes, of a perspective of Paul beginning with a theological conclusion in mind: "Hence our account of the problem will be our ultimate truth, and Jesus will arrive like a repaired tire and be fitted onto a problem that we have already worked out for ourselves."[8] We always want to avoid using Jesus to fix our theological flat tires.

---

4. See p. 25. McKnight notes that Sanders does not use the expression "New Perspective" for his work. Dunn and Wright (e.g., major proponents of the NP) do not figure significantly in Sanders's recent book *Paul: The Apostle's Life, Letters and Thought* (Fortress, 2015). Wright gets one footnote; Dunn gets three with one in-text citation. Granted, Sanders notes in his introduction that this work is meant for the "ordinary reader."

5. See p. 25.

6. Martyn's thought has deep historical roots in Germany (note Wrede, Schweitzer, and Käsemann). One quickly recalls Ernst Käsemann's famous statement: "Apocalyptic . . . was the mother of all Christian theology." See Käsemann, "Beginning of Christian Theology," *Journal for Theology and the Church* 6 (1969): 40. Martyn's essay "Epistemology at the Turn of the Ages" appears in *Theological Issues in the Letters of Paul* (Edinburgh: T&T Clark, 1997).

7. See p. 40. Campbell references Gal. 1:12: "revelation [*apokalypseōs*] of Jesus Christ."

8. See p. 44.

Finally, the *participationist perspective* offers a "prepositional" (into/ in/with) understanding of one's relationship with Christ that involves a recognition of both suffering and new life. Michael Gorman observes, "To be in Christ is to *participate* in the life of the crucified but resurrected Lord."[9] It is not simply an individual relationship, but one that participates in community vis-à-vis the church. "Justification by faith and baptism into Christ [are] participatory events of entering into life *in* Christ and *with* others."[10] Gorman notes that the perspectives need each other: "The participationist perspective should not, however, be seen as *competing with* these other views, but rather as *complementing* them."[11] Gorman frames the participationist's perspective as entering into a story: "believing the gospel (or affirming the creed) is not merely assenting to its truths but participating in its story or, more precisely, participating in the reality the story narrates."[12] Gorman observes that the event (justification) must never be separated from the story (sanctification).

Thus, each perspective is attempting to be faithfully critical to the biblical text. This must be underscored several times. This is a hermeneutical task done well with intellectual rigor and humility. It is also a vital formative task that serves both the Christian and the church.

2. *Each perspective offers a way of understanding what the perspective thinks is the main thread in the apostle Paul's theology.*

Whether it is Reformational, new, apocalyptic, or participationist, each perspective tries to unearth the apostle Paul's theological core. To return to our metaphor, different twists of the kaleidoscope certainly offer different views, yet there is some consistency of color schema and configurations. So not every interpretation is possible, just different interpretive twists.

In his understanding of the apostle Paul, Professor J. Christiaan Beker delineates the categories of contingency and coherency. He writes, "[Paul's] hermeneutic consists in the constant interaction between the coherent center of the gospel and its contingent interpretation."[13] Put simply, according

9. See p. 59.
10. See p. 63.
11. See p. 60.
12. See p. 72.
13. See J. Christiaan Beker, *Paul the Apostle: The Triumph of God in Life and Thought* (Philadelphia: Fortress, 1984), esp. "The Character of Paul's Thought," 11–19; quotation on 11.

to Beker, contingency (i.e., how to preach the Letter to the Romans) for the apostle Paul involved his creativity in relating the gospel to the particular needs of his churches. Coherency, on the other hand, is how one attempts to understand Paul's thinking vis-à-vis his understanding of the gospel.[14] This distinction is strategic for understanding how the various perspectives function. They attempt to garner the theological core of the apostle Paul's thinking.

3. The perspectives on the apostle Paul are actually perspectives on first-century Judaism(s).

Whenever one preaches or teaches from the New Testament, one is inescapably offering a certain view of Judaism. This is perhaps the lasting legacy of E. P. Sanders—not only one of the forerunners of the new perspective on Paul, but, more significantly, a forerunner of a new perspective on Judaism.[15] This also has a flip side: one of the main drawbacks to the new perspective, according to detractors, is that Judaism was inherently variegated; thus covenantal nomism is too limiting a category to understand all of first-century Judaism.[16] As a result, we were tempted to more accurately title our book *Preaching Judaisms for Christian Preachers* (not really, but you get the gist).[17]

4. Each perspective needs the others to exist.

Each perspective emerges from a reengaging of the text, using as a springboard an existing perspective's approach. In other words, each perspective

14. Of course, not all will agree with Beker's apocalyptic core to Paul's thinking. But that's just the point: the goal of the various perspectives is an attempt to uncover Paul's thought processes as he applies the gospel to his particular churches.

15. Eisenbaum notes that Sanders's book devotes 428 of its 582 pages (roughly three-quarters) to a study of Jewish literature between 200 BCE and 200 CE. Hence Sanders's book is more accurately titled *Palestinian Judaism and Paul*. See Pamela Eisenbaum, *Paul Was Not a Christian* (New York: HarperOne, 2009), 63.

16. For detractors, see *Justification and Variegated Nomism*, vol. 1, *The Complexities of Second Temple Judaism*, and vol. 2, *The Paradoxes of Paul*, ed. D. A. Carson, P. T. O'Brien, and M. A. Seifrid (Grand Rapids: Baker Academic, 2001, 2004).

17. See also J. Neusner, W. S. Green, and E. Frerichs, *Judaisms and Their Messiahs at the Turn of the Christian Era* (New York: Cambridge University Press, 1987), regarding the multidimensional nature of first-century Judaism.

has overlapping points with the others. Perspectives are not created in vacuo. One may refer to this as "synergistic" scholarship. Perhaps the best way to interpret the apostle Paul and his letters is not to assume there is only one "right" perspective, since perspectives often complement each other (I realize that there will be disagreement here). What I see as an asset of these different perspectives is the scholarly posture of a "both/and" rather than an "either/or." Scholars often establish their academic careers in an either/or milieu. This is not to suggest that all academic results are equally valid (note the current dustup with the mythical Jesus debate), but the perspectives in this volume need each other to exist, as it were. It is the scholarly gift of a "both/and" posture that offers both genuine conversations and genuine disagreements.

Conclusion

The legendary singer-songwriter-activist Bob Dylan, recent recipient of the Nobel Prize for Literature (2016), wrote a telling song in 1963, implying that there are questions of ultimate concern that may not be easily answered. One line is apropos to our understanding of the various perspectives of the apostle Paul: "The answer, my friend, is blowin' in the wind." Since the interpretive "answers" to the apostle Paul are "blowin' in the wind," one might argue, why bother in the first place? The task can seem futile and unproductive. It is in fact critical because, as in Dylan's song, these are questions of ultimate concern, and such questions are always worth the effort. We continue to interpret the letters of the apostle Paul because of their personal and ecclesiastical significance. May every interpreter continue to be faithful to this essential and weighty task.

RECOMMENDED READING

Bird, Michael F. *The Saving Righteousness of God: Studies on Paul, Justification and the New Perspective*. Eugene, OR: Wipf & Stock, 2007.

Dunn, James D. G. *Jesus, Paul and the Law: Studies in Mark and Galatians*. Louisville: Westminster John Knox, 1990.

—————. *The New Perspective on Paul*. 2nd ed. Grand Rapids: Eerdmans, 2007.

Garlington, Don. *In Defense of the New Perspective on Paul: Essays and Reviews*. Eugene, OR: Wipf & Stock, 2005.

Heilig, Christoph, Michael F. Bird, and J. Thomas Hewitt, eds. *God and the Faithfulness of Paul*. Minneapolis: Fortress, 2017.

Kim, Seyoon. *Paul and the New Perspective: Second Thoughts on the Origin of Paul's Gospel*. Grand Rapids: Eerdmans, 2001.

Mattison, Mark M. "A Summary of the New Perspective on Paul." The Paul Page, October 16, 2009. http://www.thepaulpage.com/a-summary-of-the-new-perspective-on-paul/.

Sanders, E. P. *Paul and Palestinian Judaism: A Comparison of Patterns of Religion*. Philadelphia: Fortress, 1977.

—————. *Paul, the Law, and the Jewish People*. Philadelphia: Fortress, 1983.

Thompson, Michael Bruce. *The New Perspective on Paul*. Cambridge: Grove Books, 2002.

Watson, Francis. *Paul, Judaism, and the Gentiles: Beyond the New Perspective*. 2nd ed. Grand Rapids: Eerdmans, 2007.

Westerholm, Stephen. *Perspectives Old and New on Paul: The "Lutheran" Paul and His Critics*. Grand Rapids: Eerdmans, 2003.

Wright, N. T. *Justification: God's Plan and Paul's Vision*. Downers Grove, IL: IVP Academic, 2009.

—————. *Paul: In Fresh Perspective*. Minneapolis: Fortress, 2009.

—————. *Paul and the Faithfulness of God*. Minneapolis: Fortress, 2013.

—————. *What Saint Paul Really Said: Was Paul of Tarsus the Real Founder of Christianity?* Grand Rapids: Eerdmans, 1997.

Yinger, Kent L. *The New Perspective on Paul: An Introduction*. Eugene, OR: Cascade Books, 2010.

CONTRIBUTORS

Michael F. Bird is lecturer in theology at Ridley College in Melbourne, Australia. His previous books include *An Anomalous Jew: Paul among Jews, Greeks, and Romans*; *Romans* (The Story of God Bible Commentary); and *The Gospel of the Lord: How the Early Church Wrote the Story of Jesus*, which won *Christianity Today*'s 2015 Book Award for biblical studies.

Douglas A. Campbell is professor of New Testament at Duke Divinity School and a scholar of Paul's writings. His books include *Framing Paul: An Epistolary Biography*; *The Deliverance of God: An Apocalyptic Rereading of Justification in Paul*; and *Paul: An Apostle's Life*.

James D. G. Dunn is Lightfoot Professor Emeritus of Divinity at Durham University and one of the foremost New Testament scholars in the world today. His books include *The Theology of Paul the Apostle* and the encyclopedic three-volume *Christianity in the Making*.

Timothy G. Gombis is professor of New Testament at Grand Rapids Theological Seminary. His books include *The Drama of Ephesians: Participating in the Triumph of God* and *Paul: A Guide for the Perplexed*.

Michael J. Gorman holds the Raymond E. Brown Chair in Biblical Studies and Theology at St. Mary's Seminary & University. His books include *Cruciformity: Paul's Narrative Spirituality of the Cross*; *Inhabiting the Cruciform God: Kenosis, Justification, and Theosis in Paul's Narrative Soteriology*; *Becoming the Gospel: Paul, Participation, and Mission*; and *Apostle of the Crucified Lord: A Theological Introduction to Paul and His Letters* (2nd ed.).

Richard B. Hays is the George Washington Ivey Professor Emeritus of New Testament at Duke Divinity School. His books include *Echoes of Scripture in the Letters of Paul*; *Echoes of Scripture in the Gospels*; *The Conversion of the Imagination: Paul as Interpreter of Israel's Scripture*; and *The Moral*

Vision of the New Testament: A Contemporary Introduction to New Testament Ethics.

Suzanne Watts Henderson is professor of religion and director of the Center for Ethics and Religion in the College of Arts and Sciences at Queens University of Charlotte in Charlotte, North Carolina. Her books include *Christ and Community: The Gospel Witness to Jesus* and *The Cross in Contexts: Suffering and Redemption in Palestine* (with Mitri Raheb).

Tara Beth Leach is senior pastor of First Church of the Nazarene of Pasadena in Southern California. She is a regular writer for *Missio Alliance* and has contributed to other publications such as *Christianity Today, Christian Week,* and *Jesus Creed.* She is the author of *Kingdom Culture* and a contributor to *The Apostle Paul and the Christian Life.*

Scot McKnight is the Julius R. Mantey Professor of New Testament at Northern Seminary in Lombard, Illinois. His books include *The Jesus Creed: Loving God, Loving Others; A Community Called Atonement;* and recently the International Commentary on the New Testament volumes *Colossians* and *Philemon.* He also writes the award-winning *Jesus Creed* blog at Patheos.com.

Jason Micheli is a pastor at Annandale United Methodist Church outside Washington, DC, and the author of *Cancer Is Funny: Keeping Faith in Stage-Serious Chemo.* He blogs at *Tamed Cynic,* part of the CCblogs network.

Joseph B. Modica is university chaplain and associate professor of biblical studies at Eastern University in St. David's, Pennsylvania. He is the coeditor, with Scot McKnight, of *Jesus Is Lord, Caesar Is Not: Evaluating Empire in New Testament Studies* and *The Apostle Paul and the Christian Life: Ethical and Missional Implications of the New Perspective.*

Fleming Rutledge is an Episcopal priest, best-selling author, and acclaimed preacher. Her books include *Not Ashamed of the Gospel: Sermons from Paul's Letter to the Romans; The Undoing of Death;* and *The Crucifixion: Understanding the Death of Jesus Christ,* which won *Christianity Today's* 2017 Book of the Year award.

Thomas R. Schreiner is the James Buchanan Harrison Professor of New Testament Interpretation and professor of biblical theology at Southern Baptist Theological Seminary in Louisville, Kentucky. His books include

The King in His Beauty; *New Testament Theology*; *Interpreting the Pauline Epistles*; and *Paul, Apostle of God's Glory in Christ*.

Carl R. Trueman is professor of biblical and religious studies at Grove City College in Grove City, Pennsylvania. His books include *Grace Alone—Salvation as a Gift of God* and *The Creedal Imperative*. He also writes online regularly at FirstThings.com.

Stephen Westerholm is professor emeritus of early Christianity at McMaster University in Hamilton, Ontario, and author of *Reading Sacred Scripture: Voices from the History of Biblical Interpretation* (with Martin Westerholm); *Law and Ethics in Early Judaism and the New Testament*; and *Perspectives Old and New on Paul*.

William H. Willimon is professor at Duke Divinity School where he teaches the practice of Christian ministry. He is also an editor-at-large for the *Christian Century*. His books include *Worship as Pastoral Care*; *Pastor: The Theology and Practice of Ordained Ministry*; and *Sinning Like a Christian: A New Look at the Seven Deadly Sins*.

INDEX OF AUTHORS

INDEX OF SUBJECTS

INDEX OF SCRIPTURE REFERENCES